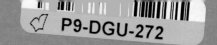

WHY HE IS A SAINT

WHY HE IS A

SAINT

SŁAWOMIR ODER *with* SAVERIO GAETA

Translated by Antony Shugaar

New York · Paris · London · Milan

First published in the United States of America in 2010 by
Rizzoli International Publications, Inc.
300 Park Avenue South
New York, NY 10010
www.rizzoliusa.com

Originally published in Italian as *Perché è Santo* in 2010 by
RCS Libri S.p.A.

This edition published by arrangement with Luigi Bernabò Associates s.r.l.,
Milan, Italy.

2010 2011 2012 2013 / 10 9 8 7 6 5 4 3 2 1

Text design by Tina Henderson

ISBN: 978-0-8478-3631-4

Library of Congress Number: 2010931722

Printed in the United States of America

CONTENTS

O Blessed Trinity, we thank you
for having graced the Church
with Pope John Paul II
and for allowing the tenderness of your fatherly care,
the glory of the cross of Christ,
and the splendor of the Holy Spirit
to shine through him.

Trusting fully
in your infinite mercy
and in the maternal intercession of Mary,
he has given us a living image
of Jesus the Good Shepherd
and has shown us that holiness
is the necessary measure
of ordinary Christian life
and is the way of achieving
eternal communion with you.

Grant us, by his intercession,
and according to your will,
the graces we implore,
hoping that he
will soon be numbered
among your saints. Amen.

Prayer for Graces Through the Intercession
of the Servant of God the Pope John Paul II

WHY HE IS A SAINT

THE UNKNOWN FACE
OF JOHN PAUL II

One day, a nun serving in the papal apartments noticed that John Paul II seemed unusually fatigued. She shared her concern with him, telling him that she was "worried about Your Holiness." "Oh, I'm worried about my holiness, too," was the pope's cheerful and immediate response. Now that the cause for the beatification of Karol Wojtyła is progressing to its natural conclusion, that concern has proved to be unfounded. His virtues—faith, hope, and charity; but also prudence, justice, strength, and temperance; and, further, chastity, poverty, and obedience—have emerged in all their dazzling completeness thanks to the testimony of those who took part in the canonical process.

It is in fact not sufficient, by the standards of the Catholic Church, to establish the so-called *fama sanctitatis* (reputation for holiness), the widespread belief among the faithful that a candidate deserves canonization. That belief was, of course, unmistakably expressed in John Paul II's case by the *Santo subito!* signs, calling for immediate sainthood, that proliferated in St. Peter's Square on the very day of his funeral. Even the required miracle—a necessary condition, considered the "seal of God"—took second place, coming into consideration only once the verdicts of theologian-consultors, the consensus of cardinals and bishops, and the signature of the new pope had certified the possession of Christian virtues to a heroic degree.

That stage of the process is reached only after a meticulous investigation by the ecclesiastical tribunal, which refuses to settle for generic declarations of esteem and veneration, however prestigious and respected the witnesses in question may be. Instead, it conducts close and thorough questioning and demands concrete evidence, detailed descriptions of specific events, and documentary confirmation—all elements that provide incontrovertible proof of the credibility of the statements. In such a context, it becomes the responsibility of the postulator—a kind of "defense attorney" for the candidate for sainthood—to bring to light the episodes that most effectively serve to certify the authenticity of the events in question.

In many cases, these are stories that have never before been told. The reason they emerge in the context of these hearings is that the witnesses—once the candidate for sainthood is dead—now feel free to recount occurrences and events that they had previously preferred to keep to themselves. The postulator is therefore entrusted with a series of reports, anecdotes, and *fioretti* (literally, "little flowers") that, when duly assembled into a larger mosaic, create a new and unprecedented portrait of the candidate.

The privilege of the role of postulator in the cause for beatification of John Paul II has fallen to me. And this book is an attempt to recount, as far as I am able, the work I did during that process.

I was born in the same part of the world as Karol Wojtyła, in Chełmża in the province of Toruń. When he was elevated to the papal throne in October 1978, I had just completed my studies at the classical high school, the *liceum*, and I was about to enter the diocesan seminary in order to fulfill the vocation to the priesthood that had been developing in my heart for the past few years. Oddly enough, though, his election as pope resulted in a delay in my consecration to God.

This was a moment of great excitement for all the Catholics of my native Poland, and I chose not to run the risk of making a life-altering decision and undertaking a momentous commitment in the midst of that collective euphoria. I felt that most human of emotions, fear, and with the approval of my spiritual director, I enrolled as a student in the Department of Business Studies at Danzig University. I lived in Danzig during the years when the Solidarity (Solidarność) movement was founded and grew, under the leadership of Lech Wałęsa. On December 10, 1981, I boarded a plane for Algiers to spend the Christmas holidays with my father, who was working there as an engineer. Three days later General Wojciech Jaruzelski declared martial law and closed the Polish borders, forcing me to remain in Algeria for the next six months.

It was a time of lengthy, intense spiritual exercises conducted in profound solitude. I returned to Poland in May 1982, and the following year I finally enrolled in the seminary, continuing my studies at the university on a parallel track. I well remember how exhausting those years were, juggling my studies and lessons and exams at both the Department of Business Studies and the Department of Theology. Then I was awarded a scholarship at the Pontifical Lateran University. I moved to Rome and began studying for my degree in canon law. My studies led to a position at the Vicariate, culminating in my present and very challenging position as judicial vicar of the court of appeal of the diocese of Rome.

The first time I met Wojtyła was on December 8, 1985, immediately after my arrival in Rome. The *cerimoniere*, or master of liturgical ceremonies, for the Holy Mass presided over by the pope in St. Peter's had entrusted me with the task of carrying the microphone for the pope's sermon. Of course, we had run through a rehearsal the day before the Mass, but I had not actually moved the microphone with its stand. When I finally found myself on the altar, uncertain whether I should move only the microphone or the entire stand, in my confusion I yanked the plug out of the jack. It wouldn't have been a serious matter, except for the fact that we were in the middle of a live worldwide broadcast. The Holy Father was standing there waiting to speak, and this thought flashed through my mind: "This is my first meeting with the pope, and it's almost certain to be my last!" Luckily, the *cerimoniere* stepped in and managed to set everything right within seconds.

A short while later, I was given another chance. The pontiff traditionally paid a visit to the seminary where I was studying for the priesthood on the occasion of the feast day of Our Lady of Confidence (Madonna della Fiducia). The rector of the seminary therefore assigned me to write and deliver a welcoming address. I spared no time and effort on that little speech, and I read it with joy, concluding with these words: "Noi abbiamo bisogno della tua fede, Santo Padre" (We need your faith, Holy Father). I turned to look at the rector, and I noted a flash of bafflement in his gaze. That's when it dawned on me what I had done. I had composed my speech in Polish, a language in which there is no difference between the formal and the informal, and then I had translated it into Italian, a bit too literally. I had used "tua" to say "your," the rough equivalent of addressing the pope on a first-name basis. For the rest of the meal, everyone made fun of me: "This is the second time that you've endangered your career: you used the informal to address John Paul II!"

I don't know if it was because of that unfortunate misstep or simply because of his extraordinarily powerful memory, but Pope Wojtyła didn't forget me. A few years later, my new bishop came to Rome for an *ad limina* visit, and he decided to take me with him for a private audience with the pope. The bishop introduced me with the fond nickname my friends used for me: "This is Father Sławek; he works at the Vicariate of Rome." John Paul II looked me straight in the eye and replied, "But when you were at the Roman seminary you didn't have a beard, did you?"

I met the Holy Father years later, in a context that appears infused with a truly remarkable significance, given subsequent events. One day, Father Stanisław, His Holiness's personal secretary, phoned to tell me that he needed to talk to me that evening. I went to the Apostolic Palace at the appointed time and, as we rode upstairs together in the elevator, he told me that I would be staying for dinner. I was speechless for a moment; I had assumed that the reason I had been summoned was simply to assign me a task of some sort. Instead, Father Stanisław accompanied me into the papal apartments where I sat waiting in the anteroom, my back to the door, when suddenly there he was, Wojtyła, greeting me and inviting me to dine with him. I was the only guest that evening.

I was seated directly across from John Paul II, with his two secretaries on either side of the table. I couldn't eat a thing, focused as I was on listening to every word of the Holy Father's conversation. He spoke with great simplicity, and exercised his unquestioned capacity to speak from the heart, one man to another. He knew that I had attended the seminary of Pelpin, and so he began to name the professors and the titles of the books they had written. Then he began to talk about his ties to the city of my youth, Toruń, where he went occasionally to pay a visit to distant relatives while he was still a cardinal. It was a wonderful encounter, but still I had no idea why he had invited me. Certainly it wasn't just a Polish get-together, of the kind that he liked to organize toward Christmas, considering that I was the only guest.

I've thought about it since then, and I now have the feeling that what led John Paul II to ask to meet me was a sort of foreknowledge, a presentiment. Perhaps he wanted to get to know a little better the man who would one day be his "representative" before the Congregation for the Causes of Saints.

On May 13, 2005, while we were waiting for the new pope, Benedict XVI, to arrive at the cathedral of St. John Lateran to address the priests of the diocese of Rome, I was asked by Cardinal Camillo Ruini, then vicar general of the diocese of Rome, to stay behind after the assembly was over. I had an airplane ticket for Poland in my pocket; I was scheduled to preside at my nephew's first Communion, and I was beginning to worry I might reach the airport too late. When I heard Pope Benedict announce that he intended to dispense with the regulation five-year waiting period for the inauguration of the cause of beatification and canonization of John Paul II, I started to suspect something was afoot.

Cardinal Ruini came directly to the point: "Did you hear what the Holy Father just said? I am very happy that you will be acting as postulator and I want to thank you for taking on the job!" I objected, pointing out that this was a position far above my abilities. Though it was true that in the late 1990s I had worked on the case of Father Stefan Frelichowski, a Polish martyr murdered at Dachau by the Nazis and beatified on June 7, 1999, I was certainly not a professional postulator. Any show of reluctance on my part was swept aside, though. After listening to my protests, Ruini replied with determination, "Thanks, and best of luck on your work." I just managed to catch my plane.

A few months later, the bishops of Poland made an *ad limina* visit to Pope Benedict XVI. My diocesan bishop asked me to accompany him, and once we were in the presence of His Holiness, he introduced me, mentioning my role as procurator. The pope congratulated me, and then added, "Work quickly, but well, in an irreproachable manner!" His recommendation has been the watchword governing my work throughout this process.

SŁAWOMIR ODER

Chapter One

THE MAN

FAITH IN FLESH AND BLOOD

During the funeral of Pope John Paul II on that sun-drenched Friday the eighth of April 2005, as the pope's former university classmate (and later cardinal) Andrzej Maria Deskur stood looking out over the sea of fluttering white banners calling for immediate sainthood—*Santo subito!*—he had a sudden flashback. In his mind's eye, he looked back sixty years to another sunny spring day, when his friend was simply known as Karol Wojtyła. It was only a few weeks since Cracow's liberation on January 18, 1945, from Nazi occupation.

With the reopening of Cracow's Jagiellonian University, one of the first signs of the return of liberty, its students had returned in great numbers to the colleges they had had to leave some years before. At the time, Wojtyła was the vice president of Bratnia Pomoc (Fraternal Help), the association of Catholic university students, which ran an extensive network of student housing. One day, Deskur, then secretary of the association, went upstairs to visit his friend. He saw that, on the door of the room where Wojtyła was studying, his friends had posted a handwritten sign: FUTURE SAINT.

Karol Wojtyła's entire life story can be told in the light of this farsighted inscription. What emerges unmistakably from the proceedings of the beatification trial is the purity and transparency of his every act, as a man and as a priest. The opinion that the world formed of him, as it got to know him better during the more than twenty-six years of his papacy, proved to be well founded. His empathy, the fervor of his prayers, his spontaneous way of talking about himself, and his ability to establish human relationships were more than mere attributes of a constructed media image. They were authentic personality traits.

We often think of Christianity as something separate from the faithful themselves, as if a life of faith were something ethereal and personal. To Karol Wojtyła, Christianity was a concrete experience, a thing of flesh and blood: the flesh and blood of Jesus Christ, who became a man in order to experience the joys and suffering of humanity. This is why Karol Wojtyła's religious testimony proved to be so remarkably fecund and influential, as documented by the numerous letters sent to the Postulatio after his death by people whom he had inspired to understand their true calling.

It is no accident that John Paul II had countless friendships. Even while he was pope, he dined with his friends, went on outings with them, went skiing with them, and organized sing-alongs and get-togethers during the traditional Polish holidays. He still corresponded frequently with his friends and never limited himself to formal, bloodless letters of platitudes. He was a genuine and deeply human individual, and his life was filled with joy, enthusiasm, and generosity, unfailingly immersed, at the same time, in an intensely spiritual atmosphere.

Like a tree—a towering, mighty oak, or perhaps the linden tree he described in the poem he wrote as a young man, "Magnificat," out of whose trunk the powerful statue of a saint was carved—John Paul II was deeply rooted in the soil of his birthplace. His homeland always claimed a place in his heart, even when, as pope, his mission embraced the whole world.

He was proud of being born in 1920, the year of the "miracle on the Vistula," the victory of the army of the newly independent Poland over invading Bolshevik forces in the Battle of Warsaw on August 15.

His father was a noncommissioned officer in the Austro-Hungarian army during the First World War; he had also taken part in the fighting against the Red Army as a lieutenant in the Polish army under the command of Marshal Piłsudski. He later proudly, and frequently, told his son Karol the story of the great Polish victory in that battle—traditionally ascribed to the Virgin Mary's intervention—and how it had halted the invading troops of Lenin and Trotsky, saving not only Poland but also all of Europe, the ultimate target of the Soviet revolutionaries.

His father, a serious man with the sense of responsibility typical of a soldier of the old guard, was a fundamental figure for young Karol, especially after the untimely deaths of his mother, Emilia, in 1929, and his elder brother, Edmund, in 1932. Karol often told his friends how deeply his soul had been stamped with the image of his father standing next to the coffin of Edmund, who had died while caring for the ill during an outbreak of scarlet fever, and repeating the words "Thy will be done!" It was with his brother that Karol had first discovered, at age eleven, what would become one of his very few leisure activities: hiking in the Tatra Mountains. After Edmund's death, it was Karol's father who took him into the mountains for long hikes together.

His family was profoundly bound up with Polish traditions and deeply rooted in the Catholic faith. The strongest influence on his spiritual formation unquestionably came from his father, but his mother, Emilia, also affected his growth as a human being, infusing his soul with a sensibility that later matured into his mystical Marianism. This religious path of love for the Virgin Mary was later marked by the remarkable personality of the tailor Jan Tyranowski, who gradually led him into an atmosphere of profound devotion and prayer.

In a certain sense, the bedrooms of John Paul II—one in the Vatican, the other at Castel Gandolfo—were shrines to the memories of his youth. Alongside photographs of his parents and his brother, set on little tables were pictures of Tyranowski and of the chaplain in Wadowice, Father Kazimierz Figlewicz, who had been Karol Wojtyła's childhood catechist and confessor.

Stripped of his last family tie when his father died in 1941, Karol experienced what might be called a broadening of the heart: his new family would be the friends of his youth and then, over time, his classmates in the seminary, his parishioners, his fellow priests, his colleagues in the episcopate, and the faithful of the Cracow diocese and of the entire world. In every place where he believed the Lord had sent him on a mission, he found substitutes for his birth family, establishing close relations with anyone he met.

"UNCLE" KAROL

Wojtyła's humanity included the traditions, the sentiments, the memories, and even the flavors of his Polish homeland. The Supreme Pontiff, for example, had a special fondness for the pastries of Wadowice, the *kremówki*, and also those of Toruń, the *katarzynki*, so anyone who visited the Vatican from Poland would bring him a freshly baked supply. Often he would refrain from eating them himself, in a spirit of penitence, but he was pleased just to be able to offer them to people who came for an audience with him.

Many was the occasion on which an event, a meeting, or a particular set of circumstances would carry him backward in time, causing crystal-clear memories to surface from his prodigious memory. The fondness he had felt for friends and classmates of his youth remained intact in his heart over the years and, more than once when he was pope, led him to get back in touch with people he hadn't seen for a long time.

That is what happened with the Jewish engineer Jerzy Kluger, a childhood friend from Wadowice days, with whom he had lost contact during the tragic events of the Second World War and the Nazi deportation of Jews to the concentration camps. After his election to the papacy, the two friends got back in touch, seeing one another frequently in the Vatican and at Castel Gandolfo until John Paul II's death. In particular, they liked to reminisce about something that happened at the end of their time in elementary school. Jerzy lived near the school, and very early one morning he went over to see the results of the admission exam for the classics-track junior high school, the *gimnazjum*. Both he and Karol had passed. Jerzy hurried to his friend's house to give him the good news, but there he was told that Karol was serving Mass in the parish church of Our Lady. Though he had never entered a Catholic church, he decided to do so that time, and waited in the back for the service to be over. From the altar, Karol noticed him, and gestured for him to stay put and not to say a word. A woman happened to recognize him, however, and asked him harshly how he dared to violate the sanctity of a church, Jew that he was. Once Mass was over, Karol joined Jerzy and paid no attention to the news that he had passed the exam. What interested him was what the woman had said to his friend. When Jerzy told him, he commented sadly, "Doesn't she know that we're all children of the same God?"

Wojtyła was only ten years old at the time, but he already took a remarkably mature view of the racial hatred that seethed in the hearts of many of his fellow citizens. That hatred would soon stoke the flames of the greatest tragedy of the twentieth century, as Wojtyła later reflected in emotional terms: "I myself have personal memories of the things that happened when the Nazis occupied Poland during the war. I remember my Jewish friends and neighbors; some of them died, others survived." It was in those years that he developed a deep respect for the Jews, and when he visited the Rome synagogue in 1986, he described them as "older brothers." That respect was emblematically validated by the pope's fond remembrance of Rome's chief rabbi, Elio Toaff, in his last will and testament—the only person mentioned other than the pope's faithful secretary, Monsignor Stanisław Dziwisz.

He was able to maintain strong ties with his classmates from his time in the *liceum*, the Polish high school. The tradition of arranging regular get-togethers, which dated back to the years in Cracow, continued after his election as pope, and on several occasions he invited them to Castel Gandolfo. When he learned during his last trip to Poland in August 2002 that the archbishop of Cracow, Cardinal Franciszek Macharski, had invited his classmates from senior year to dinner, he thanked him profusely. Later he commented, "There were forty of us, only eight survive, and not all of them were able to come."

His classmates remembered Karol Wojtyła as a friendly, talented boy, with remarkable gifts, who stood out for his elevated moral standing. In class, for instance, he refused to allow others to copy his work because he considered it dishonest.

At the same time, he was always willing to help those who needed it, explaining things they might have missed the first time or doing homework together in the afternoon. When he enrolled in the seminary, that attitude remained. When a classmate approached him to ask for help during the test that awaited them that day, Wojtyła answered, "My dear friend, trust in God and do your best on your own."

His behavior with girls was also straightforward and impeccable, as the following episode demonstrates. In 1952, Father Karol had planned a hike in the Tatra Mountains, together with two young men and three young women, to see the blooming of the crocuses. The little group was scheduled to travel by train to Zakopane on the night of April 20 and set out on their hike from there. He and the young women had already boarded the train when the boys hurried up and breathlessly informed them that the date of an important exam had been moved up and that they would have to stay behind in Cracow. For the girls, however, it was already too late to return to their school of the Nazarene Sisters; the doors were locked at ten P.M. and would not be opened again until six o'clock the next morning.

Wojtyła had only minutes to decide what to do. Caution suggested abandoning the trip—it was unthinkable for a Catholic priest to travel unchaperoned with three girls—but the absolute purity of his friendship with his three fellow hikers allowed him to say to them, "Let's go anyway." The train was crowded and there was only one seat left free. According to personal recollections, when the girls asked how they should address him in public, since it would be unseemly to call him "Father," Wojtyła, who was dressed in tourist garb, promptly replied with a well-known phrase from the writings of the Polish author Henryk Sienkiewicz, "Call me uncle." This term of address would remain his nickname to his many young friends, even when he was pope.

And that was how Wojtyła signed the letters, handwritten on letterhead stationery with the papal coat of arms, that he sent to relatives on his mother's side of the family in Toruń, to whom he was grateful for the help they had given him during the Second World War.

In those letters, he expressed his affectionate interest in the daily lives of the recipients: he asked for news of people he knew, inquired about the health of an invalid, expressed condolences for the death of a relative, and so on. He continued to monitor their well-being, to the extent that his growing pastoral responsibilities permitted. When he was a cardinal, he made a point of presiding over a number of baptisms and the wedding of a grandniece; we still have photographs of the smiling prelate at the wedding banquet. And after he became pope, he invited his relatives to Castel Gandolfo for a holiday.

Whenever he happened to be in Rome, during his time as bishop and cardinal, the Polish priests serving at the Vatican made it a rule to invite him to celebrations for birthdays or name days. Unless he had overriding obligations, Wojtyła gladly accepted. When he became pope, one of his old friends felt too shy to invite him to celebrate his name day. When that friend was invited to dinner at the Apostolic Palace one evening, John Paul II scolded him in jest: "When I was a cardinal you invited me, but now that I'm pope, you no longer invite me. Whether or not I come is a separate matter; the invitation should be forthcoming in any case!"

Indeed, many a colleague in the Roman Curia received greetings from the pope on the occasion of his name day or the anniversary of his ordination as priest or bishop. And this attentive approach was extended to laymen as well. After his election, for example, he made a phone call to Cracow asking that Maryja, the cleaning woman at the archbishop's palace in Cracow, be included free of charge in the group traveling to Rome for his consecration as pope. On the last day of his life, he bade farewell not only to the highest officials of the Vatican but also to Franco, who looked after the papal apartments, and to Arturo, the photographer who had been at his side for many years.

THE PRIEST BORN FROM
THE ASHES OF AN ACTOR

The earliest recollection of Karol's childhood was handed down by his nursery school teacher, Sister Philothea. The boy was only four years old, and was enrolled in the nursery school of the Sisters of Nazareth in Wadowice, on Lwowska Street. He was a lively, cheerful child, and the nuns called him by the nickname Lolek. Once, when he had climbed a small tree, a dog came up and started barking. The nuns were afraid the dog might bite him, and they rushed in alarm to his rescue. But the little boy seemed unfazed.

Dating to his first year in the *gimnazjum*, however, when Karol was just eleven, is an episode that clearly demonstrates his precocious, religious sensibility. At his school, there was a custodian who was a heavy vodka drinker. One day, while the custodian was walking across the street in front of the school building, he failed to notice that a car was coming. He was hit, knocked to the ground, and seriously injured. The students crowded around the injured man, unsure what to do. After a few minutes, the local parish priest arrived, accompanied by young Karol, who had hurried off to summon him to provide the custodian with spiritual assistance.

The high school years that followed were when Wojtyła discovered the theater, his first true love. At school in Wadowice, he already had given evidence of his acting abilities when he recited Cyprian Kamil Norwid's *Promethidion*, winning second prize in a contest. On October 15, 1938, when he was eighteen, he organized an evening of poetry with his classmates in the Polish philology course at the Jagiellonian University. After reciting some of his own poetry, he publicly declared his intention of becoming an actor.

A few months later, he began to frequent the Theater of the Living Word, under the direction of Mieczysław Kotlarczyk, who helped him to refine his diction, fine-tune his timing, and improve his rapport with the audience. In June 1939, he played the role of Taurus, one of the signs of the zodiac, in the play *Cavalier of the Moon*, which was performed in the courtyard of the Nowodworski prep school. He later played the role of Gucio in the romantic comedy *Maidens'*

Vows, by Aleksander Fredro. His exceptional memory, which reinforced his unmistakable talent as an actor, allowed him, during the staging of Juliusz Słowacki's tragedy *Balladyna*, to play two roles, his own and that of a cast member who had fallen ill.

During the Nazi occupation, clandestine performances continued. One day, showing extraordinarily steady nerves, Wojtyła continued reciting Adam Miciewicz's epic poem *Pan Tadeusz* (*Sir Thaddeus*) while an SS roundup was under way in the street outside.

Such love for the stage coexisted in Karol with an intense spiritual quest: two demanding paths that, sooner or later, would confront him with a difficult choice. That quandary, in all likelihood, came to a head during a production in which Karol delivered a monologue of King Bolesław the Valiant, with an evocation of St. Stanisław's resurrection of Piotrowin, and a number of excerpts from Słowacki's *The Spirit King*. An eyewitness recounted that during the first performance Karol spoke his lines with a strong and confident voice; in a subsequent performance, fifteen days later, he barely whispered the words. Asked the reason for this surprising change in interpretation, he replied that he had thought it over and had come to the conclusion that the monologue was actually a confession.

His friends decided that in this two-week period a priest had been born out of the ashes of an actor. One of those friends, after Wojtyła had already become pope, wrote a letter to him to say so, enclosing a recording of that performance. The pope responded, "What you wrote rings true.

That's exactly what happened. I agree wholeheartedly." His last appearance on stage was in March 1943, in the lead role in Słowacki's *Samuel Zborowski*.

The powerful spirituality driving this young student with a passionate love of theater certainly did not pass unobserved by his classmates at the university. One of his fellow students, who later became a close friend, testified that his discretion was so great that for a long time they didn't even know his surname. His classmates nicknamed him Sadok, after Father Sadok, the protagonist of Władysław Jan Grabski's popular novels *In the Shadow of the Church* and *Confessional*.

In those months, Wojtyła did something that could have cost him dearly. Since 1936, it had been traditional for the university youth to make an annual pilgrimage to the sanctuary of the Black Madonna of Jasna Góra. During the Nazi occupation, the pilgrimage was banned. But in order to keep the tradition unbroken, Karol managed to make his way into the sanctuary in secrecy with two other delegates, despite the fact that Częstochowa was surrounded by Hitler's troops.

UNDERCOVER IN THE SEMINARY

John Paul II often said that he attended his first seminary at home, with his father. But it was the tailor Jan Tyranowski who enlightened him concerning the deeper significance of prayer and who strengthened his sense of devotion to the divine. Tyranowski was, among other things, the founder of the Living Rosary group, made up of fifteen young people, each of whom was assigned the daily recitation of one of the mysteries. Karol joined the group, and in this school of spirituality he had occasion to read and study the *Treatise of True Devotion to Mary* by the French saint Louis-Marie Grignion de Montfort, as well as the mystical works of the Spanish saint John of the Cross.

At the age of twenty-two, however, Wojtyła came to the understanding that his path was leading him to a genuine seminary, the seminary of the archbishopric of Cracow. A few years earlier, he had resisted the call of the Lord despite direct urging by the archbishop, Adam Stefan Sapieha. On May 3, 1938, the archbishop had traveled to Wadowice for a pastoral visit to the Parish of the Presentation of the Blessed Virgin Mary and to preside over the confirmation of the students of the *liceum*. It was a Polish tradition for confirmation candidates to add a second name to their own on that occasion, and Karol chose the name Hubert in memory of the playwright Hubert Rosztworowski, who had died just a few weeks earlier and whose work Karol deeply admired.

"My religion teacher, Father Edward Zacher, chose me to give the address of welcome," John Paul II later recalled. "It was the first time I had the opportunity of being in the presence of that man who was so highly regarded by everyone. I know that after my speech the archbishop asked the religion teacher what course I would be taking upon completion of secondary school. Father Zacher replied: 'He will study Polish language and letters.' The archbishop apparently replied: 'A pity it is not theology.'"

It would be four more years before Karol's vocation found full expression. That was an event that, as he himself later put it, "remains a mystery, even to me. How does one explain the ways of God? Yet I know that, at a certain point in my life, I became convinced that Christ was saying to me what he had said to thousands before me: 'Come, follow me!' There was a clear sense that what I heard in my heart was no human voice, nor just an idea of my own. Christ was calling me to serve him as a priest." He was welcomed to the seminary by the rector, Father Jan Piwowarczyk, who urged him to preserve absolute secrecy, even with his nearest and dearest. The situation, in fact, was truly precarious.

Beginning on the first of September 1939, when Hitler's army invaded Poland, the seminary building had been requisitioned to house the SS unit in charge of security for the occupation forces in the city of Cracow. For the first few months, the seminary students had been moved to lodgings on the third floor of the archbishop's palace. But once the Nazi occupying governor ordered all educational institutions closed, Archbishop Sapieha distributed some of the students to the various parishes as assistants while the rest of the students, assigned to work for companies placed under the control of the German authorities, would continue their studies at home. These undercover seminary students knew nothing about one another. Textbooks for their studies of philosophy and theology were delivered to them directly from the prefect, Father Kazimierz Kłósak; each student then took his exams on a one-on-one basis with the professor.

For two years, from the autumn of 1942 to the summer of 1944, Wojtyła was a member of this second group. In order to avoid being deported to Germany for slave labor, he needed the vital German *Ausweis*, a pass issued by the German authorities to workers deemed "useful to society," and so he too—after a brief stint as a delivery boy for a restaurant—had taken a job in 1940 in the stone quarry of Zakrzówek, half an hour's walk from his house in Debniki, as assistant to the man who set off the explosive charges in the quarry.

In the spring of 1942, he took a new job at the Solvay chemical plant in Borek Fałęcki, where he was in charge of purifying the water in the boilers. Here he continued to work while undertaking his studies as a clandestine seminarist. His fellow workers always saw him with a book and, thinking that he was a university student, covered for him, allowing him to study on the job.

His spiritual director was Father Stanisław Smoleński, who considered him gifted with a great intellectual and moral foundation, and who appreciated how willing Karol was to sacrifice and to work hard. Karol was sustained by a sturdy constitution, which enabled him to overcome the accident that occurred on February 29, 1944. Hit by a truck on his way to work, he was left unconscious at the side of Konopnicka Street and only regained consciousness in the hospital, with a bandaged head.

At the beginning of August 1944, Karol left his job at the Solvay plant in response to the summons of Archbishop Sapieha. When the Warsaw insurrection began, the archbishop had ordered all the seminary students to return to the archbishop's palace on Franciszkańska Street. He justified this step with the Nazis by saying, "I have a few seminary students staying with me because, as archbishop, I have a right to have someone to help me serve Mass."

Karol arrived at the seminary dressed in a white shirt and a pair of cotton trousers, with clogs on his feet. The following day he received a cassock, a donation from a diocesan priest. The ten or so seminarians were initially given lodgings on the second floor of a side wing of the palace, with windows overlooking an inner courtyard and Wiślna Street. In October, after the Warsaw uprising was crushed, the archbishop offered their rooms to priests who had fled the capital, moving the entire group of seminary students to the audience hall, next to his own suite of rooms. The young men slept on metal cots set close to one another, and attended lessons in the same area.

The days were busy. They woke every morning at five, performed their ablutions, and then exercised in the atrium, followed by prayer in the chapel and meditation. The metropolitan celebrated Mass, then they breakfasted and attended lessons in philosophy and theology. At one o'clock, they had lunch, then were free to walk in the inner courtyard. After that came adoration of the Holy Sacrament, study, and spiritual readings. Dinner was at eight, then religious service in the chapel, followed by silent pursuits. At nine, the metropolitan went into the chapel for an hour of adoration, which he performed prostrate on the chapel floor before the Eucharist, and at ten o'clock he returned to his apartment, looking in on the seminarians in the audience hall to make sure they were asleep.

One fellow student recalled that what struck him about Wojtyła was "above all his kindness, his benevolence, and his sense of comradeship. He conversed easily, did his best to understand, and discussed subjects that were of interest and importance to each of us. He spoke sparingly and listened more than he talked; occasionally, he would make a discreet observation. In any case, he never imposed his views on others and never hurt anyone's feelings with offensive words. He had a serene gaze, he was witty and cheerful, and he liked to listen to funny stories that made him laugh. He observed the rules of the seminary faithfully. During lessons he was focused, taking diligent notes and getting the teacher's point rapidly. At examinations he was clear and direct; his responses met with his professors' approval and aroused the admiration of us all."

THE PHANTOM OF
THE DOUBLE HOMICIDE

Harking back to this dramatic period is a defamatory accusation that was leveled against Wojtyła by the radio and television journalist Marco Dolcetta in his book *Gli Spettri del Quarto Reich* (The Specters of the Fourth Reich), published in Italy by BUR in November 2007. Let us reconstruct the story that Dolcetta tells, which leaves a significant number of questions unresolved.

In the context of an investigation into the last gasps of Nazism at the end of the twentieth century, Dolcetta reports that he interviewed a certain Horia Sima, the leader of the Romanian Legionary Movement (Iron Guard) in 1938 and deputy prime minister of Romania between 1940 and 1941. Sima later became a secret agent reporting to Heinrich Himmler, the chief of the Nazi police forces, and infiltrated the ranks of the Polish resistance movement on behalf of the Gestapo and the SS. The interview, "preceded by waverings, fears, and second thoughts," took place in Madrid in an unspecified month in 1978. It is, however, no longer possible to check these statements with Sima: he died on May 25, 1993, in Madrid.

During the conversation, Sima showed Dolcetta a sheet of paper with a few terse phrases in German, which translate as: "Secret Notes of the High Command. Chief Reich Security Department. General Division. Multiple statements confirm that a Polish Catholic priest, Karol Wojtyła by name, took active part in the murder of Germans. He committed the crime with a knife. I hereby order that the murderer's name be entered on the list of individuals wanted for arrest. To implement said recommendation contact the Cracow Gestapo directly. Department F. VII A. Sent by SD I and II Gestapo I RSM 87."

A shocking revelation, which Sima explained to the Italian writer with these words: "In Cracow, we maintained special surveillance of the city's archbishop, Prince Adam Stefan Sapieha, because of the extreme freedom with which he engaged in anti-German activities. After a series of meetings with the local clergy, in which I passed myself off as a

Hungarian refugee, a high school teacher, and a Catholic, wanted by the SS, I learned about the undercover organization operating under Church protection. . . . Sunday, August 7 [1944] was the day of major Gestapo roundups throughout Cracow. I was in Gestapo headquarters going over the lists of potential terrorists. When I saw the name of Karol Wojtyła I had a strong reaction, because he was a very religious young man, kept under special observation because he was thought to be the son of a Jewish woman, Emilia Katz, naturalized with the Polish name of Kaczorowska, and because he was friends with young Jews, whom he protected."

The account continued with the appearance of a second protagonist, Grigori Caratiniescu, one of Sima's collaborators: "Caratiniescu, who had got a good look at the conspirators, moved around Cracow in the company of two officers of the Gestapo, all three in civilian clothes. Wojtyła lived in the center of Cracow, and Caratiniescu identified him as he was returning home with two other young men. Before they could stop them, the three young men ran off. They followed them, but Caratiniescu couldn't keep up with the Poles and the two Germans who were chasing them. He saw them run off and then, on turning a corner, he saw the bodies of the two Germans on the ground, bleeding. There was no sign of the three fugitives. . . . The next day, the two wounded officers died. It was learned that Wojtyła had been given shelter in the palace of Prince Sapieha, the archbishop, and that Sapieha had given cassocks to him and twenty other Catholic subversives, and that he hastily made them clerics. . . . I was astonished, but only somewhat astonished, many years later, when he was elected pope. This was only a further confirmation of my views on the Vatican."

If we link this last statement with the date claimed for the interview, 1978, a first suspicious contradiction emerges. Wojtyła was elected pope on October 16. Unless the interview happened to be conducted in the last couple of months of that year, it would be impossible for Sima to refer to his election. But if it was, then his reference to the distant past ("when he was elected pope") for an event that in theory occurred no more than a few weeks earlier is stranger still.

It seems all the more incomprehensible that, at the very moment that the world's attention was focused on the newly elected Wojtyła, both Sima and Dolcetta should have failed to exploit a piece of information that, if it were true, would have been a spectacular scoop. Equally noteworthy is Dolcetta's perseverance in keeping this journalistic bombshell to himself for some thirty years, and then dropping it casually into the story on page 155 of his book. Moreover, we should point out a significant detail that certainly undermines the accuracy of this historical reconstruction: in 1944, the date mentioned, August 7, actually fell on a Monday!

In any case, it is evident that an accusation of such gravity naturally led the Postulatio for the cause of John Paul II to take active steps to ascertain the truth of the matter. When questioned about the case, the most respected source on this subject, the Commission for Contemporary History, with headquarters in Bonn, issued over the signature of Doctor

Karl-Joseph Hummel the dry reply that "since 2003 there exists a microfilm edition of all available documentation and reports of the state secret police, of the head SD office of the SS and the head office of Reich Security from 1933 to 1945: this edition does not contain the document in question, and the name Wojtyła does not appear in the detailed opening volume, not even as an index entry."

Doctor Hummel was unsparing as he continued with his analysis: "A comparison of the documents in the microfilm edition with Dolcetta's document reinforces the impression that Dolcetta's document is a counterfeit, and not a particularly clever one: the heading lacks indication of date and location; the person sending the document is not identified as required and the recipient is not indicated either; the Gestapo normally knew who they were talking about and would not be likely to identify a Polish theology student as a 'Catholic priest.'" And he concludes, after explaining that he requested clarifications from the author to no avail, that "perhaps the reason for his silence is the fact that this document does not exist in the archives, and was in fact 'fabricated' at some later date."

In light of these considerations, the accusation appears wholly baseless. This explains, among other things, why despite its supposedly being a "bombshell," historians have entirely ignored it.

IN THE SERVICE OF GOD
AND OF HIS PEOPLE

In October 1946, now–Cardinal Sapieha decided to send Wojtyła to Rome to complete his studies at a pontifical university. He set the first of November, the Feast of All Saints, as the date for Wojtyła's ordination as a priest. Early that morning Karol presented himself, accompanied by a small group of friends and relatives, in the metropolitan's private chapel, where the ceremony took place.

On November 2, which Catholic liturgy dedicates to the commemoration of the dead, he celebrated his first Mass in St. Leonard's Crypt at the Wawel Cathedral in Cracow. In the days that followed, he also celebrated Mass in the parish church of St. Stanisław Kostka in Debniki and in the Church of the Presentation of the Mother of God in Wadowice. He celebrated another Mass at the altar of St. Stanisław, also in the Wawel Cathedral, for his friends from the Theater of the Living Word and for the members of the clandestine organization called Union to which he had belonged during the Nazi occupation.

His ordination was an absolutely central moment in Karol Wojtyła's life. He has emphasized that point himself, declaring that "nothing means more to me or gives me greater joy than to celebrate Mass each day and to serve God's people in the Church. That has been true since the day of my ordination as a priest. Nothing has ever changed this, not even becoming pope."

A significant testimony in this respect is provided by a monsignor who chanced to recognize a homeless person who was always to be found in Rome's Via della Traspontina, not far from St. Peter's, as a priest who had left the ministry. The monsignor managed to include the homeless man in a papal audience in the Vatican's Sala Clementina and alerted John Paul II to his presence. Once the gathering was over, Pope Wojtyła summoned the man into the adjoining hall, and sat alone with him. When the homeless priest emerged, he was in tears. The pontiff, he explained, had asked him to confess to him; after confession, Wojtyła had said, "Do you see the grandeur of the priesthood? Don't besmirch it."

On November 15, 1946, accompanied by the seminarian Stanisław Starowieyski, Father Wojtyła boarded the train that would take him across the Polish border for the first time. It was a long and emotional journey, as he recounted: "From the window of the moving train I looked at cities known only from my geography books. For the first time I saw Prague, Nuremberg, Strasbourg, and Paris, where we stopped as guests of the Polish Seminary on Rue des Irlandais. We soon departed, since time was pressing, and reached Rome in the last days of November." He first stayed with the Pallottine Fathers, then moved permanently to the Pontificio Collegio Belga (Pontifical Belgian College) on Via del Quirinale, just a short distance from the Pontifical University of St. Thomas Aquinas (Angelicum), where less than two years later, on June 19, 1948, he took his degree with a dissertation entitled "Doctrina de fide apud S. Ioannem a Cruce" (The Doctrine of Faith According to St. John of the Cross).

For Father Karol, the audience that he had in early 1947 with Pope Pius XII was a deeply moving experience. The pope greeted individually all of the young priests and seminarians of the Collegio Belga, and when he came to Father Karol, the rector Maximilien de Furstenberg introduced him and said he came from Poland. Pius XII stopped and, with evident emotion, repeated the words "from Poland" and then said, in Polish, "Praise be to Jesus Christ."

Dating from that period was a conversation that Wojtyła had with a Belgian priest active in the Jeunesse Ouvrière Chrétienne (Young Christian Workers), founded by the future cardinal Joseph Cardijn. Together they discussed the situation that had developed in Europe in the aftermath of the Second World War, and the Belgian priest said to him, "The Lord allowed the experience of something as evil as Communism to befall you—and why did He do that?" The Belgian went on to answer his own question: "We in the West were spared that experience, perhaps because we would not have been capable of withstanding such an ordeal. But you will succeed." That is a phrase that John Paul II would later recall for its prophetic significance.

One of his classmates recalled that period: "Napoleon's maxim 'I may lose a battle but I should never lose a minute' was frequently mentioned in our Collegio Belga. Wojtyła took advantage of every minute to complete his dissertation. We knew that he was a talented soccer player, but we couldn't persuade him to become the captain of our team. Was that why we lost our matches against the Brazilian and English teams? In any event, every once in a while he would come and play with us in the little games we held in the garden."

WITH HIS ARMS EXTENDED
IN THE SIGN OF THE CROSS

Karol was intensely focused on his goal. As a classmate from his time in Rome emphasized, "He was always very discreet when he was with friends, and the group photographs provide proof of that. He can always be seen in the back row. In conversation, he was never notably eloquent. I would not have imagined that, a few decades later, he would speak with such confidence and would become such an energetic and effective leader of the universal church. His case appears to me to be a demonstration of the French saying 'The job makes the man.'"

With many of these friends, he fell out of touch for a number of years, but he insisted on seeing them all again in the Vatican not long after his election as pope. He invited them to celebrate Mass together in his private chapel, and then to dine with him. As one of those present recalled, John Paul II cordially said, "I know you all by first and last name. Who could have thought that I would have to become pope for us to get together again after thirty-one years?"

A few days after defending his thesis, Wojtyła returned to his diocese, where he was assigned his first working position—what the Polish call the *aplikata*—as assistant parish priest in Niegowić, about twenty miles east of Cracow. Niegowić was a community of five thousand people scattered among thirteen villages and hamlets, entirely isolated from the larger network of public transportation. On July 8, 1948, Father Karol boarded a bus leaving Cracow. At a certain point, he had to get off and proceed on foot. Then a farmer gave him a ride on his wagon. When they reached the border of his new parish, he asked the farmer to stop. He got down and knelt to pray for all his new parishioners, following the example of St. Jean-Baptiste-Marie Vianney, the famous Curé d'Ars.

For a year, he worked alongside the parish priest Kazimierz Buzała and three other vicars. At the same time, he taught religion in five elementary schools scattered through the countryside, for about thirty hours a week, and also supervised the Catholic Girls Association. To speak in simple words, to work hard, frequently in the face of challenging social and economic conditions, and to live in a rural environment that was so different from his academic background constituted a genuine pastoral challenge for an intellectual like Father Karol.

The parishioners were deeply impressed by his extraordinary Eucharistic devotion, which was manifested in long sessions of adoration of the Most Blessed Sacrament. It was not uncommon for Wojtyła to spend part of the night in prayer before the altar, stretched out on the floor, his arms spread in the sign of the cross. As one eyewitness put it, "The presence of Christ in the tabernacle allowed him to have a very personal relationship with him: not merely to speak to Christ, but actually to converse with him." After observing the behavior of the young chaplain for a time, his housekeeper prophesied: "You will become a bishop."

In October 1948, Cardinal August Hlond died, and the Polish church chose a young archbishop, forty-seven-year-old Stefan Wyszyński, to replace him as primate. The episcopate was determined to bring to bear its most effective forces in the battle against Communism, to combat the spread of Marxist ideas. In accordance with this general policy, on August 17, 1949, Cardinal Sapieha decided to transfer Father Karol to the Parish of St. Florian in Cracow, located not far from the Jagiellonian University.

The parish priest, Monsignor Tadeusz Kurowski, put him in charge of the catechesis of the upper classes of the *liceum* and gave him pastoral responsibility for the university students. Wojtyła invited the university students to a weekly Thursday session on crucial questions about spirituality and the existence of God—powerful topics in a general environment choked with Communist propaganda promoting militant atheism. In order to better illustrate his thoughts—which often involved subtle theological issues—he prepared outlines and had them mimeographed on newsprint.

It was in this university setting that a circle of close friends developed who spent holidays together and, in a number of cases, later became married couples. And it was on the foundation of the conversations of that period that Wojtyła's theology of the human body and of marriage took shape and definition. His well-known book *Love and Responsibility*, published in 1960, was originally the text of spiritual exercises that he suggested for engaged couples.

On their first excursion, to the village of Kozy, the group slept in the parish church of Father Franciszek Macharski, who later replaced Pope Wojtyła as archbishop of Cracow. This was the beginning of a long series of outings, which often involved travel by kayak. Every morning Mass was celebrated, and, after the reading from the Gospels, there was a short sermon featuring a phrase upon which the group was to reflect for the rest of the day. Father Karol loved spending time with people, but he also loved those kayak trips because, paddling by himself or with at most one companion, he had the luxury of thinking and reflecting in perfect freedom. It was a source of great joy for him when, in the year 2000, a group consisting of three generations of those long-ago friends came to see him at Castel Gandolfo for what was dubbed "dry kayaking." They presented John Paul II with a canoe on the lawn of Castel Gandolfo, they sang songs in honor of their "uncle," and after the ceremony no fewer than 120 people greeted him one by one.

To get the young people in his parish involved, Father Karol also had the idea of founding a choir, which began with five boys and the same number of girls. The first musical repertoire they put together was a selection of *Kolędy*, the Christmas hymns of which Poland has such a rich tradition. Then the young assistant parish priest asked his actor friend Jan Adamski to lend a hand, and he managed to stage a Lenten mystery play, produced in church during the Easter season of 1951.

TOTUS TUUS

Father Karol's activism and his cultural background made an impression on Archbishop Eugeniusz Baziak, who had become the religious leader of Cracow after Cardinal Sapieha's death on July 23, 1951. Baziak decided to push him toward university teaching, and so in September 1951 Wojtyła began studying for the examinations to qualify as a lecturer in ethics and moral theology. He received his certificate in December 1953, with a thesis entitled "An Evaluation of the Possibility of Constructing a Christian Ethics on the Basis of the System of Max Scheler." As luck would have it, his teaching certification was the last issued by the Department of Theology of the Jagiellonian University. A few months later that department was suppressed by the Communist authorities.

Father Karol immediately began teaching, at the Seminary of Cracow and the Catholic University of Lublin, until he was formally appointed on November 15, 1957, as an untenured lecturer. To show the importance he attributed to this office, suffice it to say that from 1967 on—when as cardinal he no longer had the freedom to travel physically to Lublin—he taught the lessons in the archiepiscopal residence, paying for the students to travel to Cracow out of his salary as professor.

Alongside his teaching duties, he continued to look after his young people, well aware that direct involvment in pastoral activities was much more than an "extra," and in fact constituted the very essence of his calling as a priest. It was, therefore, no accident that the official notification of his appointment as auxiliary bishop of Cracow should reach him while he was out on one of his regular summer excursions, in July 1958. His summons to an audience with the cardinal primate Stefan Wyszyński had been communicated to him some days previously. And so Father Karol had left his cassock with a friend in Warsaw before he nonchalantly set out, wearing a light shirt and shorts, in a canoe to paddle the Łyna River.

On July 3, 1958, he left the group and, accompanied by his friend Zdzisław Heydel, landed not far from the village of Olsztynek. He was able to hitch a ride on a truck loaded with sacks of flour and get to the railroad station, where a late-night train was scheduled to leave for Warsaw. He had his sleeping bag with him but, as he recalled later, "there was no need, because I did not sleep a wink." On July 4, he appeared punctually at the bishop's palace on Miodowa Street, and Cardinal Wyszyński informed him of the decision of the Holy See. Wojtyła was ready with an objection: "Your Eminence, I am too young, I've just turned thirty-eight." The primate answered ironically, "That is a shortcoming of which you will rid yourself soon enough. I beg you not to resist the will of the Holy Father." Wojtyła had no choice but to accept.

The following day he traveled to Cracow to inform Monsignor Baziak and to ask permission to return to his friends at the campsite on the Łyna River. At first, the archbishop resisted, explaining that it struck him as inappropriate, but Father Karol argued, "What about the fact that it's Sunday? Who will say Mass for them? It will be a privation." At that point, Baziak yielded, and sent him off with a smile: "Go on, then. But please come back in time for your consecration!"

The rite was scheduled for September 28, the liturgical feast of St. Wenceslaus, patron saint of the Wawel Cathedral. The ceremony called for a number of symbolic gifts to be offered in the name of the newly consecrated auxiliary bishop by persons close to him. Six friends brought the candles, bread, and wine. "I didn't have a family, I had you," Wojtyła later said to those he had chosen as "representatives." The celebration continued in the seminary, where the guests were welcomed for a frugal reception, and it concluded in the sanctuary of Częstochowa. There, at dawn, Wojtyła celebrated Mass for his closest friends in the chapel of the miraculous icon of the Black Madonna.

It was in honor of the Virgin Mary that he chose to have his episcopal crest bear the motto "Totus tuus," inspired by the doctrine of St. Louis-Marie Grignion de Montfort. These are the opening words of a sentence in which the saint expressed his will to belong entirely to Jesus through the medium of the Virgin Mary: "I am all yours, and all that I have belongs to you, O most loving Jesus, through Mary, your most holy Mother."

As the bishop explained, "This saint's teaching has had a profound influence on the Marian devotion of many of the faithful and on my own life. It is a *lived teaching* of outstanding ascetic and mystical depth, expressed in a lively and passionate style that makes frequent use of images and symbols." An old friend of his, Cardinal Andrzej Maria Deskur, confirmed: "His devotion to the Virgin Mary certainly directed my life to a great degree. Already in Cracow he explained to me the significance of the holy slavery of St. Louis-Marie Grignion de Montfort. He used to say that we must serve God the way that Mary did, in a state of complete abandonment."

ALL IN THE LIGHT OF FAITH

For four years, Wojtyła was a tireless assistant, in every aspect of the episcopal ministry, to Archbishop Baziak, who was weakened by illness. After Baziak's death, it was therefore natural that the chapter of Cracow elected him to serve as vicar capitular until the Holy See should name the new diocesan authority. In reality, the senior auxiliary bishop was Monsignor Julian Groblicki, and during the assembly of July 16, 1962, Wojtyła had stressed that point in urging that Groblicki be chosen. But the chancellor of the curia, Monsignor Kuczkowski, an impressive figure, knelt before Wojtyła and begged him, in the name of the needs of the church of Cracow, to accept the office of vicar capitular.

Three months later, on October 5, Monsignor Wojtyła left for Rome to take part in the first session of the Second Vatican Council, from October 11 to December 8, 1962. He repeated the journey the following year, from October 6 until December 4, on the occasion of the second council session, and afterward traveled as a pilgrim to the Holy Land from December 5 to December 15. Even as he retraced the earthly footsteps of Jesus Christ, he was aware that just two weeks later, on December 30, 1963, his appointment as archbishop of Cracow would be made public.

There was immense joy in the diocese, and on March 8, 1964, when his solemn consecration was celebrated in the Wawel Cathedral, many of the faithful were unable to enter the overcrowded church. There was an equally intense wave of warmth toward him a few years later, during the celebration of the Sacrum Millennium Poloniae (Poland's Sacred Millennium) in 1966. Wojtyła celebrated Mass in the parish church of Szczepanów, birthplace of the bishop and martyr St. Stanisław, patron saint of Poland. In an outpouring of love and enthusiasm, the faithful carried him in their arms from his automobile to the altar.

A funny story is told about the millennium celebration in Tum Łęczycki that year. It was raining heavily, and water had filled the baldachin over the altar. Someone tried to relieve the weight of the water by lifting a corner of the awning, but misjudged the angle, and all the water poured onto the archbishop, who nonetheless maintained a demeanor of imperturbable stoicism.

With his auxiliary bishops, who grew in number to four in April 1970—besides Groblicki there were also Stanisław Smoleński, Jan Pietraszko, and Albin Małysiak—Wojtyła established a collegial working style, with a weekly meeting during which they could talk over the current issues. These problems, he emphasized from the outset, were to be addressed first of all from the point of view of faith. Joining the group, on each occasion, were the directors of the various diocesan offices, such as the chancellor, the notary, or the various directors.

One of his auxiliary bishops testified that "in his episcopal ministry he took inspiration from the pastoral models of

St. Stanisław, who was martyred in order to defend his people against the abuses of the Polish king Bolesław, and St. Charles Borromeo, his patron saint, the bishop of the reformations of the Council of Trent. In the light of those examples, Wojtyła distinguished himself in his courageous defense of the Polish people against the Communist dictatorship, supporting their right to religious freedom and liberty of worship."

In Cracow, as one witness recounted during the beatification process, the archbishop "invited to his home the various social groups: intellectuals, professionals in the cultural and academic sectors, lawyers, and health providers. In that way he encouraged and reinforced, offered support, and provided ideas. On all these occasions he took the opportunity to speak, so that everyone who attended these very well organized meetings would have something to remember from them. He was a very good speaker, and he had a highly developed sense of humor."

Even while he was bishop he continued to devote special attention to his pastoral duties to the young, whom he saw as the great hope of the Church. This ministry, he said, was in his blood, and in fact he never neglected it at any time in his life. He worked to provide young people with spiritual guidance, maintaining personal contacts and spending time in conversation with them. He was aware of the fundamental importance of catechesis, and he urged priests to set up special courses for all age groups, until the teaching of religion was again allowed in the public schools.

THE LESSONS OF VATICAN II

Wojtyła was much involved in the work of the Second Vatican Council. After taking part in the first two sessions, he also attended the third (September 14–November 21, 1964) and the fourth (September 14–December 8, 1965). The archbishop spoke during the assembly a total of eight times, submitted thirteen written memos, and contributed to three more with other priests at the council. He was a member of the Commission for the Study of Population Growth, the Family, and the Birth Rate, and he took an active part in the subcommittee entrusted with the drafting of the working document, Schema XIII, that would serve as the foundation of the pastoral constitution, *Gaudium et Spes* (Joy and Hope). This was a fundamental experience for him, and it later bore fruit in the form of the book *Sources of Renewal: The Implementation of Vatican II*, written to impress upon his own priests and the faithful at large the importance of incorporating the council doctrine in the ordinary pastoral care of the diocese of Cracow.

He focused in particular on three topics: the Church, freedom of religion, and the contemporary world. Addressing the ecclesiological question, Wojtyła suggested that, in the final draft of *Gaudium et Spes*, the chapter on the people of God should come before the chapter on the Church hierarchy, showing the high consideration he felt for the community of the faithful. A consideration that—at a time when many saw the lay community as little more than simple executors of the decisions made by the ecclesiastical hierarchy—Wojtyła expressed through minor gestures as well. Speaking during the debate on the apostolate of the laity, for instance, he began with a sonorous "Venerabiles patres, fratres et sorores" (Venerable fathers, brothers, and sisters); he was thus the only speaker to publicly emphasize the presence at the council of a number of women attending as auditors.

On the topic of religious freedom, his remarks highlighted, on the one hand, how faith can never be the target of coercion on the part of the civil power and, on the other, that entrusting freedom of faith to personal responsibility does not mean opening the door to religious indifferentism.

Wojtyła left his deepest mark, however, on the outline of the relationship between the Church and the contemporary world. Working on the draft of the document, he offered a series of observations on the excessively moralistic tone of the text and the placement of the Church at too high a remove from the world. In the section of the document that he edited, there is a rather forceful insistence on identifying atheistic Communism as a fundamental problem facing the contemporary Church. The subcommittee, however, rejected his text, considering it excessively focused on atheism.

The theologian Yves Congar was asked to rework the text, which, amid lively discussions, he turned into the fourth chapter of *Gaudium et Spes*. We can now read in *Mon Journal du Concile* (My Council Diary) the notes that Congar—created cardinal by John Paul II in 1994—made at the time: "Wojtyła made a very strong impression. His personality is imposing. It radiates a magnetism, an attraction, a certain prophetic force, very calm but indisputable."

In a critique of the final draft, in the speech that he made to the assembly on September 28, 1965, Wojtyła raised two objections. First of all, he underscored the absence of Christian realism in the vision of the world set forth in the text and criticized the facile optimism of those pages. Second, with reference to atheism, he declared that "it would be appropriate to distinguish between atheism that springs from personal convictions and atheism that is imposed from outside with pressures of all kinds, physical and moral, especially when it becomes impossible to profess one's own faith in public and official life, and one is almost forced to profess atheism, so that the education of the young is steeped in atheism, even when the parents are opposed."

In the end, not even the slightest reference was made in the council documents to the question of Communism (in the index of the Second Vatican Council, the term never appears). A silence that the archbishop deeply regretted.

RECONCILING CULTURE AND
PASTORAL DUTIES

Within the Polish Episcopal Conference, of which he was vice president, Karol Wojtyła worked especially on cultural relations with the universities and the pastoral care of the laity. As chairman of the Episcopal Commission on the Laity, he did everything within his power to ensure that, in accordance with the wishes of the Second Vatican Council, the lay faithful could take on important tasks in the life of the Church.

He certainly expended an equal effort on ensuring cultural enterprise and raising the academic standards of theological studies in the diocesan seminaries: he saw this as the only way to prepare competent professors for theological universities. At his initiative, the so-called Academic Board was established, under his personal supervision.

A man of deep and vast cultural learning, Wojtyła not only urged the professors in the theological institutes of higher education to produce books on the challenges of the contemporary world, but he himself also wrote scholarly articles that were published in a number of Polish periodicals. He devoured books, taking every opportunity to read and keep himself informed. In order to be able to read in the car, he had a special reading lamp mounted on the backseat. One anecdote has it that, while on holiday, a woman read aloud to him from one book, and her daughter read to him from another, while he was reading yet another book at the same time.

In Cracow, he worked in the chapel on Franciszkańska Street, where he was able to study and pray without excessive distractions (to maintain concentration, he sometimes read with his feet immersed in cold water). Many people remember seeing him kneeling at his desk, which still stands to the left of the tabernacle. Prayer was always a source of strength and inspiration for him, to such a degree that even during the interval between one lesson and the next at the seminary he would hurry to the chapel for a quick spiritual reinvigoration.

In the mid-1950s, the Polish government suppressed the departments of theology at the state universities of Warsaw and Cracow, replacing them with the Academy of Catholic

Theology in Warsaw, with the intention of undermining the power of the Catholic Church. Wojtyła and Cardinal Wyszyński held differing opinions about this institution. Wyszyński, who had worked hard to ensure that the teachings of the academy should remain within the precincts of Catholic orthodoxy, and who was fairly happy with the result, considered it in any case a tool at the service of the Church. Wojtyła on the other hand opposed recognition of the academy by the Holy See. Although he too acknowledged its doctrinal orthodoxy, he did not want an institute financed by the Communist regime to be seen as a legitimate successor to the two university departments that had been suppressed, fearing that such a move might forfeit the right of the Church to have a university theology department of its own.

As General Wojciech Jaruzelski, former president of the Polish Republic, publicly admitted, "We often made comparisons between Primate Wyszyński and Cardinal Wojtyła. We used an image, describing the primate as the 'rock' and Wojtyła as the 'icebreaker,' in the best sense of the term, that is, as a man capable of shattering prejudices on both sides of the divide."

The Communists did their best to foment disagreements between the two churchmen, saying that Wyszyński was rigid and fanatical, while Wojtyła was an educated, open-minded man. For that very reason, Wojtyła allied himself forcefully and openly with Wyszyński to prevent the possibility of any misunderstanding. The authorities gradually realized it was not true that Wojtyła was more willing than Wyszyński to resolve problems through compromise. And they had definitive confirmation in September of 1967 when, after the primate was denied a passport to take part in the first general assembly of the Synod of Bishops in Rome, Wojtyła decided not to attend either, in a gesture of solidarity.

His relations with Cardinal Wyszyński were extremely loyal. When he spoke about the primate, Wojtyła described his remarkable personality and emphasized his gift for keeping the Polish episcopate united at a particularly trying time for the Catholic Church. The first responsibility of the episcopate of any nation, he frequently said, is to preserve its unity, as that ensures the survival and vigor of a church. For that reason, any disagreements that existed would get relegated to the background (a likely reference to differences of opinion between him and the primate) in order to safeguard unity among the bishops.

Still in the context of obviating conflict and encouraging reconciliation, we should mention an initiative in which Wojtyła played a strong and leading role, and which aroused indignation and controversy. This was the drafting of the well-known letter sent on November 18, 1965, by the Polish episcopate to the German episcopate as a symbolic gesture of peaceful reconciliation between two nations so bitterly opposed during the Second World War. The text included a line from Horace that had been used by Pope Paul VI in his letter dated September 29, 1962, to the separated brothers of the Catholic Church: "Veniam damus petimusque vicissim" (We forgive and seek to be forgiven in return).

In spite of the hostile propaganda mounted by the Communist authorities and the difficulties that many Polish Catholics felt in accepting a gesture of such scope, in the end the initiative certainly had a positive and constructive outcome. With the benefit of historical perspective, we can look back and see in this courageous decision an early manifestation of what would be distinctive traits of Pope John Paul II: the desire to overcome the wounds of the past, to encourage reconciliation among peoples, to look to the future with a new spirit.

Cardinal Wojtyła was also, during a trip to West Germany in September 1975, the first of the Polish bishops to choose to visit East Germany, as a small but significant gesture of encouragement toward a church that was struggling with profound isolation and daunting challenges posed by the oppressive Communist regime. Wojtyła traveled to Erfurt, where a large Catholic gathering was under way. There he presided over the Eucharistic celebration and met with the bishop, later cardinal, Joachim Meisner, with whom an enduring friendship was born.

IN THE CHILL OF NOWA HUTA

In order to encourage the involvement of all the priests of the Cracow diocese, Archbishop Wojtyła established the presbyterial council, a body that he always consulted before making any important decision. The council was made up of thirty priests, chosen democratically out of the entire clergy every four years. One of the members declared that "from the very beginning, he placed great trust and reliance in the council, as an expression of the same trust shown by Christ toward the Church and its ministers. Wojtyła always presided over the

Mass that marked the beginning of every council meeting, commenting upon the word of God, and then moderating the debate. The atmosphere that developed during the work was cordial, serene, and fraternal. Anyone was free to speak, with the knowledge that his opinion would be heard with gratitude and interest." And in fact the presbyterial council gave rise to a number of initiatives promoting the education, cooperation, and collaboration of the priests, which the archbishop always approved wholeheartedly.

Wojtyła considered dialogue fundamental. When faced with a problem, first he engaged in an in-depth analysis of the situation, then he consulted with those who might help him to find a solution. He never said, "It can't be done, it won't succeed," but instead, "Let us see how we can do it." When he presided over a meeting, he always began with an invitation to lay out the question "as it appears in the light of faith."

Those who turned to him for advice always found in him serious and focused attention. A bishop who had been appointed to a prestigious new position asked him, "You know me well. What should I do to perform my new ministry effectively?" Wojtyła took time to find an appropriate answer and then said, "That is the same question that I asked in a similar situation of a superior of mine, and he answered simply, 'Be yourself.' That is the same thing that I now say to you."

Another answer that he often gave to those who asked him what decision they should make was: "Have you thought about what your vocation is?" A witness who recalled this answer was one of his students from his university pastoral duties in Cracow: "When a number of politicians started a hunger strike, I turned to Wojtyła, who was our spiritual adviser, and asked him what I ought to do. His answer was simple: 'Have you asked yourself exactly what your vocation is? You may be summoned to be a father, a teacher, a politician. If you can find a persuasive answer to that question, then you will know what to do!'"

In order to encourage the renewal of the life of the local church, he paid pastoral visits to the parishes almost every Sunday. In the speeches that he made on those occasions, he was fond of repeating St. Augustine's phrase "Vobis sum episcopus, vobiscum christianus" (I am a bishop for you, I am a Christian with you).

With a style that was exquisitely personal, Wojtyła did not limit himself to celebrating Mass and delivering a sermon when he made these visits, but instead he placed the central focus on a meeting with different groups of the faithful who belonged to that parish: children, young people, students, intellectuals. He would bless the married couples, so that they would support one another in all the circumstances of life on earth and help one another on the path to salvation. And if there were sick people who had been unable to make it to the church, he would go to visit them in their homes, or in the hospitals or nursing homes, where he spoke words of encouragement to the physicians and the nursing staff as well.

He was especially tenacious in his efforts to encourage the construction of new churches in his diocese, an objective that was clearly at odds with the aims of the regime. The case of Nowa Huta was emblematic. According to the plans of the Communist government, this new quarter for the working class was to be the first city built without God. But the archbishop was certainly not willing to let that happen, and he continued to support the project to build a house of God, setting an example with his actions—for instance, celebrating a Christmas Mass there at midnight, in the open air, under the roof of the stars. In the end, the church was built, to the great joy of the faithful, who gathered tearfully, more than fifty thousand of them, to witness the consecration on May 15, 1977.

This was an episode in which we see, in Wojtyła, not only his crystalline determination to pursue his goals, but also his ability to exercise judgment above and beyond any preconceptions and received ideas. The archbishop in fact chose to entrust the duties of builder-priest to Father Józef Gorzelan, who had already performed a similar task in Filipowice. And he did so despite vocal opposition and objections about the priest's fitness to hold that duty, prompted by the fact that Father Gorzelan was a member of Caritas, which in Poland was a state-run charitable organization and did not enjoy the approval of the Polish episcopate.

When Archbishop Agostino Casaroli—the chief supporter of the Vatican's Ostpolitik, the policy of cautious openness toward the regimes of Eastern Europe—visited Poland, the Polish authorities showed him that they had issued permits for the construction of sixty churches (actually just small chapels in little villages). Wojtyła then invited the guest from the Holy See to come to Krowodrze, where the Church of St. Jadwiga Queen of Poland now stands. It was November, and a wintry mix of rain and snow was falling. Together they celebrated Mass in a shack that could hold some fifty people, while at least ten times that number stood outside. When a thoroughly chilled Monsignor Casaroli returned to Warsaw, he paid a call on the Communist authorities and expressed his intense displeasure at the way they had misled him on the real need to build new churches.

Wojtyła was always on the front line when it was a matter of defending the existence of the Church and protecting the properties that were indispensable to supporting its mission. In 1962, rumors circulated that the authorities were planning to expropriate the seminary building on Manifestu Lipcowego Street and transform it into a student center for the Graduate School of Education. The archbishop, first of all, pronounced an act of consecration to the Madonna to entrust to her the fate of the seminary. Next, he ordered the seminarians to make an early, unplanned return from the spiritual retreat in which they were engaged. He then informed the authorities that, when they came to seize the building, he would make sure that all the canons were in front of the building, waiting for them. There was no more talk of state expropriation.

Entirely unprecedented for the diocese was the care that Wojtyła devoted to unmarried mothers. This was a decision that never failed to incur the disapproval of older priests, irritated at help being provided to persons they considered "at fault." By offering this help, they objected, weren't they running the risk of justifying bad behavior? Wojtyła was decisive in his reponse that what he was doing was essentially safeguarding innocent children (and there were more than fifteen hundred of them).

In 1974, the cardinal contacted Sister Bernarda Krzecz-kowska, the provincial superior of the Sisters of the Holy Family of Nazareth, suggesting that she take over the management of the home for unwed mothers. The nun did not conceal her concerns from Wojtyła. "What will happen if the maternal instinct is awakened in some of the younger nuns and they therefore leave the congregation?" she asked. The archbishop reassured her: "That's a risk we run, Mother. But I know that this is something of God's, and you will see that what you fear will not happen." Indeed, as the nuns later saw, no sister ever left the congregation for that particular reason and, quite the contrary, since then the number of vocations has only grown.

The first unwed mother arrived at the home on Warszawska Street on November 4, 1974. Word spread rapidly, and soon many young—and less young—women began to arrive from every corner of Poland. Wojtyła in fact had specifically instructed the nuns to welcome all pregnant women, without exception, no matter what part of the country they came from. In 1978, the facility was becoming too small to accommodate all the unwed mothers. And so, shortly before the cardinal entered the Conclave, the superior, Sister Cherubina Zofia Bokota, came to see him in the company of the provincial mother to ask what she should do. The answer was to buy another building. The home was moved to Przybyszewskiego Street 39, and Wojtyła offered a substantial down payment out of his own pocket, while the rest of the sum came from the treasury of the diocesan curia.

As pontiff, he likewise made the defense of life one of his priorities. A witness at the process of beatification recalled that one day John Paul II, while they were discussing this issue, gave him a penetrating look and raised one hand high in an extremely forceful gesture. Then he proclaimed: "We must take every imaginable action against the abominable crime of abortion." The man froze: in that gesture and in that glare was the same energy that had inflamed his words of condemnation against the Mafia in the Valley of Temples in Agrigento, Sicily, and the same determination with which he had resisted the heckling of the Sandinistas in Nicaragua while he was celebrating Mass.

IN THE SIGHTS OF THE
POLISH INTELLIGENCE SERVICE

A powerful and authoritative personality like that of Karol Wojtyła could hardly pass unobserved by the Polish authorities, who focused the eyes of the Intelligence Service of the Secret Police upon him. The historical commission of the process of beatification reconstructed carefully the phases and the dynamics of this surveillance campaign over the years, working in collaboration with the archives of the Polish Institute of National Remembrance in Cracow and in particular with the researcher Marek Lasota, who in 2006 published a book on the subject titled *Donos na Wojtyłę: Karol Wojtyła w teczkach bezpieki* (Denouncing Wojtyła: Karol Wojtyła in Polish Communist Secret Service Records).

The first sign of interest on the part of the Communist regime toward Karol Wojtyła actually dates back to May

1946, when his name appeared on a list compiled by the third section of the regional office of State Security (WUBP) in Cracow: "Wojtyła Karol, resident of Podzamcze Street 8, son of Karol and Emilia, born on May 18, 1920, cleric by profession, student of theology in Cracow." Next to that entry are the handwritten initials of Jan Sikora, the bureaucrat assigned to carry out the analysis of the young seminarian's personality.

A few years later, at the end of 1949, an agent using the pseudonym of Zagielowski reported the observations he had made of the Parish of St. Florian in Cracow. "I have determined the approximate appearance of the 'Circle of Altar Boys' of Father Kurowski," he wrote, among other things, "which operates in the Parish of St. Florian. I have not been able to determine whether it has been registered. Their director is Father Kurowski himself, now replaced by a new vicar, Father Wojdyla [sic], and before that by Father Obtulowicz. The meetings last as long as two hours, they read reports, and they play parlor games."

For the time being, the interest of the Intelligence Service appears to have remained fairly limited, and there is not another notation until January 17, 1956, when the director of the Office of Religion of Cracow reported a conversation "with Dr. Father Karol Wojtyła, already professor at the Catholic University of Lublin and at a number of seminaries." In conclusion, he noted: "Concerning his work and his relationship with the social movement of the Catholic progressives, he says that he does not want to meddle in those matters because he prefers to steer clear of them. Karol Wojtyła is a fervid executor of papal excommunication in the matter of

Piasecki's *Zagadnienia Istotne*, as well as the magazine *Dziś i Jutro*, which he has never read and continues not to read. He has never sworn an oath of allegiance to the People's Republic of Poland."

The reference was to the periodical founded on November 25, 1945, by the association Pax, which consisted of the so-called Catholic progressives who were in favor of the transformation of the Polish state into a socialist system. The mastermind of the project was Bolesław Piasecki, who in his book *Zagadnienia Istotne* (Essential Problems), published in December 1954, had identified a Catholic framework for the changed social conditions. Six months later, the Holy Office had placed on the index of forbidden books both that book and the magazine *Dziś i Jutro* (Today and Tomorrow) because of the false information that they provided concerning the situation of the Catholic Church in Poland and the muddling of Catholic doctrine with Marxist ideology. The Holy See, however, thanks to the intervention of Monsignor Klepacz, who served as interim president of the Polish Episcopal Conference during the internment of Cardinal Wyszyński between 1953 and 1956, decided not to excommunicate Piasecki and his association.

Following Wojtyła's appointment as auxiliary bishop of Cracow on July 4, 1958, the interest of the authorities grew exponentially, as is demonstrated by the massive volume of documents about him. Two things emerge from this material. One is the unmistakable interest on the part of the Intelligence Service in monitoring the bishop's contacts with the Cracow cultural circles that opposed the regime. The other is the major effort put in place to hinder his work. Among those notes one can read, for instance: "Ever since the late fifties, Wojtyła has been active in the organization of the laity, especially among the educated class and the young. He has managed to gather around him many experts and colleagues. He organizes numerous conferences, gatherings, and congresses, as well as meetings with groups of intelligentsia and of young people. Wojtyła has earned great respect from the bishops and the parish clergy, but especially among the Catholic activists." In particular, Wojtyła was a supporter of the Klub Inteligencji Katolickiej (Club of Catholic Intellectuals), which was especially powerful in Cracow but had branches in all the major cities of Poland and constituted a pole of attraction for many lay intellectuals as well.

At the beginning of the 1960s, under the heading F Group, the Intelligence Service set up a special unit devoted to the constant surveillance of Bishop Wojtyła. The instructions to the operatives were very specific: "You must monitor systematically all the official speeches given by the subject on the occasion of ecclesial celebrations, both in the Cracow city area and in the diocese. Afterward you must judge the speeches from the following points of view: the subject's interpretation of the changes in our country (political, economic, and cultural changes); the attitudes suggested to the faithful for the catechesis of young people and adults, for the implementation of the Great Novena project, et cetera; whether in any of the speeches in question there are negative references or even just allusions to the people's authorities."

The interest of the authorities was not limited to surveillance of Wojtyła's public activities but extended to scrutinizing

his private life as well: "You must carry out systematic observation of the contacts entering the private apartment of Bishop
Wojtyła. Do so after receiving the signal from Department T
concerning planned meetings. Continue observation at all
hours of the day. Making use of the assistance of the Office
of Religion of the National Council of the city of Cracow and
of the Department for Politics of the National Council for the
old city, establish a formal charge in the deliberative council for the fact that he hindered inspection of his apartment.
Make use of the visits of the rental board with the failure to
comply with the obligation despite a written warning."

Following the death of Archbishop Baziak and the election of Wojtyła as vicar capitular, the Intelligence Service
cracked down even harder. At the time, the appointments of
bishops were supposed to receive the approval of the Polish
authorities and so, repeatedly, the ecclesiastical representatives had informally submitted to the Communist official in
charge of religious matters, Zenon Kliszko, lists of potential
candidates. The name of Karol Wojtyła was marked off in a
corner, but Kliszko said that the Communist Party would
prefer him: in fact, they thought that he had no interest in
political matters, but was rather a scholar, a philosopher. "A
man of dialogue" is how Kliszko described him to Cardinal
Wyszyński, remembering a negotiation that he carried out
with the auxiliary bishop concerning the Cracow seminary.

The officers of the Polish Secret Police thought differently,
and expressed to the political operatives their strong opposition
to the appointment of Wojtyła: "The reasons that argue against
his candidacy: Bishop Wojtyła is unreservedly engaged in the

actions of the Church. Since he is a particularly gifted person with a great talent for organization, he is the only bishop who would be able not only to consolidate the members of the curia and the diocesan clergy but also to attract a substantial portion of the intelligentsia and the young Catholics, among whom he enjoys considerable respect. Unlike many other diocesan administrators, he is on easy terms with monasteries and convents, which are numerous in the territory of the archdiocese. Despite his apparent elasticity and openness to compromise in his contacts with the state authorities, he is an especially dangerous ideological adversary."

Meanwhile, the Holy See had also become active, sending Monsignor Franco Costa, a personal friend of Pope Paul VI and general ecclesiastical assistant of the Azione Cattolica Italiana (Catholic Action), to carry out a confidential investigation in Poland. Upon his return, Costa reported that he had been deeply impressed by the spiritual substance and the cultural erudition of the young Bishop Karol Wojtyła. His words to Pope Montini were more or less these: "Poland does not have only Cardinal Wyszyński. It also possesses impressive younger bishops, such as Wojtyła, who are certainly worth as much as the primate."

Wojtyła must have had some inkling of what was going on around him. This is indicated by a remark he made at the end of a letter he sent to Padre Pio da Pietrelcina on December 14, 1963, when he was in Rome for the Second Vatican Council: "At the same time, I venture to submit to you the immense pastoral difficulties that my poor efforts encounter in the present situation."

The outcome we know: Karol Wojtyła was named archbishop of Cracow. The Intelligence Service was therefore obliged to intensify its operation, and Wojtyła began to be kept under surveillance even when he traveled abroad. The analysts of the Polish United Workers' Party (PZPR) drew up this concise summary of his work in Rome: "Thanks to his active participation in the preparation of the council documents, the contents of the speeches delivered during the sessions of the Second Vatican Council, and his work on the council commissions, he was appreciated in the Vatican as well. This certainly led to the development that, in June 1967, Wojtyła by a papal appointment became a cardinal."

He was elevated to the rank of cardinal by Pope Paul VI on June 28, 1967. From that point onward, the archival material becomes more voluminous each year, indicating the Polish authorities' awareness that Wojtyła was now the leading figure in the Catholic Church of Poland as well as the most dangerous adversary facing the Polish Communist regime.

In the documents, we find an assortment of fairly thoroughly reasoned judgments about his personality and his actions, in which it is possible to detect a vein of thinly disguised admiration on the part of the writer: "He is unanimously described as a talented, hard-working, ambitious person. He is considered one of the more intelligent bishops, a clear thinker possessed of sound judgment. In his private life he is outgoing, straightforward, and modest. He does not flaunt the dignity of his ecclesiastical position and his vast learning. He is not particularly interested in material things. He reads a great deal. He has not been noticed trying to imitate others. In his actions, he always relies on his own analysis of conditions. With respect to the clergy, the cardinal has proven to be an energetic diocesan administrator willing to try new ideas, and at the same time he is tractable and open-minded."

A FIERY SERMON

The archbishop was never reluctant to comply with government requests for meetings. Indeed, he took advantage of those meetings to display the moral strength that he felt he possessed. We can see a fine illustration in this note drafted by the director of the Office of Religion: "This is Wojtyła's first personal contact with the regional authorities. I never saw him 'in action.' I can therefore say something about him in comparison with others. Wojtyła was trying to be a little different from the ones we already know (Jerzy Karol Ablewicz, archbishop of Tarnów; Jan Jaroszewicz, bishop of Kielce) by maintaining a degree of spontaneity in his demeanor and attitude. That is to say that from the beginning of the meeting he made an effort to settle comfortably in his chair, resting his chin on his thumb; he tried to make all his movements relaxed and completely natural. Perhaps he wanted to stress his own confidence, he wanted us to understand that he was an important, influential man. At the same time, he was very straightforward. He smiled constantly in a slightly benevolent manner. And he showed great freedom in his thinking. He was in no hurry to give his answers, which were clear and logical."

The power of his reasoning put the Communist officials in serious difficulties when they were required to reply to him on matters regarding the diocese. Even the delegation chief of the Office of Religion, Kąkol, was obliged to acknowledge this during a meeting in Poland with the Vatican nuncio Luigi Poggi in the mid-1970s. During Wojtyła's cause for beatification, an eyewitness recalled that "in one of the breaks in the meeting Kąkol, speaking about certain Polish bishops, said of Wojtyła that when he wrote to the authorities, it took sweat to respond with adequate arguments."

Lucid and incontestable, the words that the archbishop leveled against his institutional interlocutors were sometimes charged with an unusual and overwhelming energy. This once happened during a pilgrimage to Kalwaria Zebrzydowska at the beginning of the 1970s. As one witness has recounted, Wojtyła delivered on that occasion his fieriest homily against the Communist rulers, subjecting them to a pitiless criticism. During the trip back to Cracow, he was asked, "What happened, Father Cardinal? This is the first time I have heard you so heated." Wojtyła replied, "During the Mass I felt a force enter into me, an imperative to which I could not answer 'no.'" A force that, from that moment on, would always power his homilies and sermons, giving the Polish authorities a good few reasons for concern.

The regime knew very well who it was dealing with. One of the countless analyses composed on the subject of Wojtyła by the Communist functionaries in the mid-1970s said, "Our analysis of the workings of the Roman Catholic Church in Poland allows us to state that, for the past several years now, the church of Cracow occupies a leading position, so that the main power in the supervision of the life and activity of the Church in Poland is increasingly being held by the command center in Cracow. While absolutely not demonizing the person of the metropolitan archbishop of Cracow, we must admit objectively that his wisdom and the authority that he enjoys consist, among other things, in the magnificent capacity to make use of the scholarly potential that the church of Cracow has at its fingertips, both through the Catholic organizations and with the support of leading personalities in the city's academic circles."

When Wojtyła was elected pope in 1978, the documentation about him that the Intelligence Service transmitted to the Ministry of the Interior in Warsaw filled no fewer than eighteen cartons. In dealing with such an unexpected development, a number of analysts from the Political Office read that material with a fairly naïve and optimistic mindset: from the top of Vatican Hill, they argued, the view is much broader than from Cracow's Wawel Hill. Their hope was that Cardinal Wojtyła, once he became pope, would shift his focus to the world at large, and that this would allow him to glimpse the glaring shortcomings of capitalism and the misery of the underdeveloped parts of the world, thus shifting his opinion about the values of Communism. A hope that proved utterly vain.

The Polish Intelligence Service stubbornly continued its surveillance throughout the 1980s, intensifying its spying during the pontiff's trips to Poland in 1979 and again in 1983 and 1987. Two years later, all that paper would be tossed aside by the impetuous winds of history.

THE BELLS OF POPE PAUL VI

When in June 1967 a letter arrived from the Vatican announcing that he had been appointed cardinal at the express wishes
of Pope Paul VI, Wojtyła was performing a pastoral visit. The
chancellor informed him of the letter's arrival, and the archbishop returned to the curia, opened the envelope, read the
letter, then set it on his desk and stood bowed over it for a
long time, without speaking a word. At last, the chancellor
asked him whether the letter was confirming the rumors that
he had been named a cardinal, and he replied, "Yes, but one
can also refuse the appointment." The chancellor replied that
one could not go against a decision made by the Holy Father.
At that point, everyone offered him their best wishes and con-
gratulations, and he asked them all to pray. Upon his return
from Rome, his only comment was "On my back I carry the
gift for the archdiocese."

The relationship between Wojtyła and Pope Paul VI was
a long-standing one, based on sentiments of mutual respect
and deep-seated affection. As early as 1962, during the first
session of the Second Vatican Council, the auxiliary bishop
had had the opportunity to thank then-cardinal Giovanni
Battista Montini for the generous gift that the archdiocese
of Milan had given to the collegiate church of St. Florian in
Cracow: three new bells, blessed with the eloquent names
Virgin Mary, Ambrose–Charles Borromeo, and Florian. They
had been requested by Father Tadeusz Kurowski, rector of St.
Florian, but Wojtyła knew perfectly well that Montini meant

them as an expression of his personal goodwill toward him, one of the youngest bishops in the world.

A few years later, in 1968, Wojtyła was one of the few bishops who was clearly aligned with Pope Paul VI when he began his reflection on the topics of marriage and procreation, and he went so far as to establish in Cracow a committee for further study of the matter, which provided the pope with a number of ideas to counter the position of those who wished to soften the Church's stand on contraceptives. And when Pope Paul VI issued the encyclical *Humanae vitae* in July 1968, reaffirming the unacceptability of artificial methods of contraception, Wojtyła prepared a memorandum on the encyclical's doctrinal and pastoral consequences that was published in the *Osservatore Romano* on January 5, 1969.

At the beginning of February 1976, a phone call from the future cardinal Władysław Rubin informed Wojtyła that the pope wished him to lead the Lenten spiritual exercises in the Vatican. There were only about twenty days available in which to prepare the texts for the exercises, so the cardinal moved to the convent of the Grey Ursulines in Jaszczurówka. Until noon he wrote his meditations (later published in book form with the title *Sign of Contradiction*), each afternoon he went skiing, and in the evening he resumed his writing.

That experience, Wojtyła himself recalled in his book *Wstańcie, chodźmy!* (*Rise, Let Us Be On Our Way*), "was particularly important for me, because it made me realize just how necessary it is for a bishop to be ready to speak of his faith, wherever the Lord asks this of him. Every bishop needs to be prepared for this, including the successor of Peter himself, just as Paul VI needed me to be ready and willing for the task." On November 1, 1993, John Paul II wrote to Marek Skwarnicki: "There is controversy over Christianity, Jesus himself, and his Gospels. I myself have a certain predilection for being a 'sign of contradiction,' even if it is through no merit of my own, but by grace."

One official of the Roman Curia who was present at those spiritual exercises testified that "Wojtyła had the courage to 'engage in polemics' with the pope. In particular we can detect this in the lecture on Gethsemane, in which he expressed the solitude of Pope Paul VI. The cardinal 'polemicized' in the following manner: he described the opportunity that the Apostles lost in the olive garden to respond to Jesus' prayer and urged Pope Montini to do his best to regain that lost possibility. Little did he realize that two years later he himself would have to respond to that challenge."

When Pope Paul VI died on August 6, 1978, Cardinal Wojtyła sketched to a group of friends a prophetic picture of the needs of the Church: "It seems to me that the Church, and the world as well, needs a very spiritual pope. This must be his first and indispensable characteristic, so that he can be the father of a religious community. Asia, Africa, and Latin America are struggling with new and difficult situations, and they will seek a successor to Pope Paul VI who can help them and, more important, understand them in their time of difficulty."

THE PROPHETIC "HABEMUS PAPAM"

The Conclave began on August 25, 1978. In the last Mass celebrated before entering the Sistine Chapel, the cardinal recited
this prayer: "We pray to you, Almighty Father, that, if a man
is elected pope who realizes that he is not strong enough to
bear the weight of the responsibility that comes with the task
of serving as vicar to your Beloved Son, you will infuse him
with the courage to say, in the words of St. Peter: 'Go away
from me, Lord, for I am a sinful man!' But if he does take on
this responsibility, give him a great store of faith, hope, and
love, so that he can bear the cross that you impose upon him."

The decision of the cardinals to elect the Venetian Albino
Luciani, who took the name of John Paul I, was wholeheartedly
endorsed by him: "I believe he is the the ideal man, with his
piety and humility, susceptible to the action of the Holy Spirit.
This is the pope that the Church needs today." But little more
than a month later, during the night of September 28–29, Pope
Luciani died as well.

Wojtyła later said of him: "His words deeply touched the
hearts of the people crowding into St. Peter's Square. From
his first appearance in the central loggia of the basilica of the
Vatican he established a current of spontaneous sympathy
with those present. His smiling face, his open, trusting gaze
won the hearts of the Romans and the faithful of the entire
world. His words and his person entered into the souls of one
and all. With his sudden death, there was extinguished the

smile of a Shepherd who was close to his people, who with serenity and equilibrium managed to establish a dialogue with culture and with the world."

Józef Mucha, the driver for the archbishopric of Cracow, was the one to deliver the news of the death of John Paul I. The cardinal was seated at the breakfast table, and when he heard those words, uttered by the man through the opening between the kitchen and the dining room, he was seized by a powerful wave of intense emotion, and he dropped the spoon he was holding onto his plate. A short while later, a severe migraine forced him to cancel the trip that was scheduled for that day. He went into the chapel to pray, and to the members of the secretariat he said thoughtfully, "What is the Lord trying to tell us with this?"

Before boarding the plane that would take him back to Rome, on October 3, 1978, Cardinal Wojtyła completed a visitation to a parish in the archdiocese of Cracow, the Parish of St. Joseph in Złote Łany, a new residential quarter of Bielsko-Biała. Upon his return, he celebrated a Suffrage Mass for the late pope, and then went to Warsaw for the proceedings of the Polish Episcopal Conference. He finally left for the Vatican "without the knowledge that I was going there to stay," as he later commented. As if in a presentiment, when the driver who took him to the airport wished him a safe and timely return home, he replied in a serious voice touched with sadness, "One never knows."

On October 14, Wojtyła once again entered the Conclave. Two days later, at 5:15 P.M. on October 16, 1978, he was elected the 263rd successor to St. Peter, the first non-Italian since the death of the Dutch Pope Adrian VI in 1523. A few hours before that, Cardinal Wyszyński had reminded his confrere Léon-Etienne Duval, archbishop of Algiers, that this was the feast day of St. Jadwiga, Queen of Poland, and therefore suggested that he vote for the cardinal from Cracow. He then described the cardinal: "He is a mystic, a poet, a shepherd, a philosopher, a saint . . . but he is a bad administrator," referring to the difficulties that he had encountered, in Wyszyński's opinion, less in the management of material concerns than in the organization of the curial government.

At the moment of his election, Wojtyła must certainly have been reminded of the prophecy uttered by Cracow's archbishop Eugeniusz Baziak the day that he had gone to inform him that he had been appointed his auxiliary bishop. Baziak had taken the young Father Karol by the arm and led him into the waiting room, where a number of priests were sitting. He had then announced in a strong voice: "Habemus Papam."

Immediately after his election, another of his onetime teachers and mentors, the rector of the Pontifical Belgian College, Maximilien de Furstenberg, since created cardinal, sent John Paul II this significant message of good cheer: "Magister adest et vocat te" (The Teacher [Jesus] is here and is calling you). The pontiff replied, "Obeying in faith to Christ, my Lord, placing my trust in the Mother of Christ and of the Church, despite these great difficulties, I accept." Words that set the seal upon his entire papal ministry.

Chapter Two

THE POPE

THE SECOND HOME OF THE POLES

On October 16, 1978, for the first and only time in the history of the People's Republic of Poland, the evening news report did not begin punctually. When the anchorman finally appeared on the screen, his face pinched in an expression of tension and embarrassment, everyone watching understood that something extraordinary had happened, something that had taken the Communist authorities by surprise. Attempting to minimize, however awkwardly, the historic scope of the event, the announcer informed the Polish people of the election of Karol Wojtyła to the papacy. The black-and-white picture on the television screen, so much a part of the memory that most Poles have of that event, suddenly seemed colored with hope. People, still incredulous, threw open the doors of their apartments and went to ring their neighbors' doorbells: "Did you hear what's happened?" In the street, people were running about and hugging jubilantly, a festive exchange of good wishes while church bells were pealing in unison.

One witness testifying in the process for beatification recalled, "With my girlfriend and a few friends, we had decided to go to the movies that evening. But that news report changed our plans, and we were soon at the parish church exulting, embracing one another, and celebrating." Everyone wholeheartedly rallied around their fellow Pole, who had been elected by the cardinals of the whole world as the man best suited to steer the Church toward the third millennium of the Christian era.

In the years to come, for many Poles the Vatican would become the ideal second home of their nation, a welcoming space in which to share moments bound up with their national traditions, with their homeland, especially during the Christmas season. For the students of the Pontifical Polish College, the old friends from Cracow, and fellow Poles working in the Roman Curia, it was customary to celebrate with the pontiff the ceremony of the *Opłatek*, in which season's greetings are exchanged by breaking a special nonconsecrated wafer. "The appointment was made with the unfailing phone call from Father Stanisław: 'This afternoon the pope wants you all to come over to sing Christmas carols,'" recalled one of the most assiduous participants in those get-togethers. "We met in the private library, in a comfortable family atmosphere. John Paul II would sit down and we would gather around him. Then we would begin singing in chorus and he, with his beautiful voice, would naturally take the lead part. There was a sort of lullaby that he liked a lot, and he loved to invent new verses for it, adapting it to the particular situation and the people who were present."

The guests all knew that this invitation was not simply a gift that John Paul II reserved for those people who were dear to him: deprived from a very young age of all family ties, he actually needed the feeling of a family's warmth around him, a family made up of people with whom he had established deep and lasting ties. In some sense, this also explains the number of personal references that the pope scattered throughout his speeches for the entire duration of his pontificate, confidences that have made it possible to retrace a genuine "autobiography of the heart," published in 2008 by the Vatican Publishing House, titled *Vi racconto la mia vita* (*Let Me Tell You About My Life*).

A POLE ON ST. PETER'S THRONE

It is not at all easy to summarize a papacy like that of John Paul II, the third longest in history, with its nearly twenty-seven years. Let us attempt to do it with the description provided by one of his closest friends: "The most important moments can be broken up into four phases. The first is that of the enthusiastic papacy, the pope who travels new paths, who is familiar with the reality of the world, who ventures out of the Vatican and makes contact with the entire Church. The second phase consists of the assassination attempt, his illnesses, his suffering, his recovery in the hospital, his bearing of the cross. The third phase is when he was hung upon the cross, immobilized and confined to a wheelchair. The fourth phase was his death, which had a paschal dimension, and was an integral part of his entire life."

Certainly, John Paul II's pontificate represented a clear break from the past—a break that was evident from the very beginning—when he called into question the tradition of the papal coat of arms, deciding to keep the one he had as archbishop, with a large cross on a blue field and an M in the lower right quadrant, symbolizing the Madonna at the feet of the crucified Jesus. Experts in heraldry were appalled, but there was nothing to be done. The pope did not even want the papal tiara above his coat of arms: he would allow at most a miter. Here, however, the insistence of officialdom, with a steady stream of notes about historical tradition and what is appropriate, managed to dent Wojtyła's determination, and he agreed to use the tiara.

Equally astonishing was his decision to go, the day after his election, to visit Monsignor Andrzej Maria Deskur at the Gemelli Polyclinic, where he was a patient. That the pope, behaving like an ordinary mortal, should go to see a sick friend (which he had previously done on October 14, before entering the Conclave) on the occasion of his first official sortie from the Vatican was an absolute break with tradition and ceremony, a decisive shift that furrowed more than a few brows. Those who knew him well, however, were able to read in this act a sincere gesture of gratitude to a man that Karol Wojtyła would ever afterward consider one of the *cireneos* (selfless toilers) of his papacy.

Wojtyła and Deskur first met in Cracow in 1945, when they were both officers of the association of Catholic university students, Bratnia Pomoc. They became closer friends in the seminary, despite the four-year age difference, and their friendship remained strong even when, after their ordination into the priesthood, Deskur was sent to the Vatican Secretariat of State to work in the field of social communications, becoming president of the Pontifical Council for Social Communications in 1973 and bishop in 1974.

For Wojtyła, Deskur thereafter became an important point of reference during his visits to Rome. He would sleep at Deskur's house whenever he was summoned to the Vatican, and he confided in him and discussed with him the projects he was mulling over. During the sessions of the Second Vatican Council, Deskur was also Wojtyła's confessor. Wojtyła promoted him to archbishop in 1980, and in 1984 he appointed him president emeritus of the Pontifical Council for Social Communications. The following year he created him cardinal.

Three days before Wojtyła's election to the papacy, on October 13, Deskur had been stricken with paralysis at home, and had been taken to the hospital with slim chances of survival. "I did not merely yield to an impulse of the heart when I went up there, to Monte Mario, to visit somebody who was a friend of mine," John Paul II explained in a speech on

December 21, 1980. "At the time I wished to give—and I can confirm this at a remove of two years—a very specific indication of the way in which I conceived and continue to conceive of the formidable ministry of the successor to St. Peter. In that setting, I said to the patients that I counted greatly, very greatly indeed, on them: for their prayers and especially for the offering of their sufferings, which could provide me with a special strength, a strength that was and is necessary to me in order to perform in a less unworthy manner my serious duties in the bosom of the church of Christ."

Deskur himself later wrote in the *Osservatore Romano* on December 11, 2003: "My suffering supports this fruitful pontificate. That is what Mary wanted, and I am her servant!" He recovered from his stroke, though he was forced to live the rest of his life in a wheelchair.

The existence of a particular correspondence, in the lives of men of faith, between suffering and the spiritual aid offered by other people through that suffering was a deep-rooted conviction for Karol Wojtyła, and the fact that his own election to the pontificate should have coincided with the beginning of a grave illness for one of his closest friends only confirmed that belief.

In a previously unpublished note dating from the days immediately subsequent to his election, we read: "I cannot fail to link the fact that on October 16 I was elected as the successor [to John Paul I] with what took place three days earlier. The sacrifice of Andrzej, my brother in the episcopate, appears to me as preparatory to this event. Everything, through his suffering, is inscribed within the mystery of the cross and of the redemption brought about by Christ. I also find a certain analogous quality in an event that occurred eleven years ago when, during my stay in Rome for the consistory at which I was summoned to join the College of Cardinals, my friend Father Marian Jaworski lost his hand in a railroad accident near Nidzica." The writing ends with the admission "*Debitor factus sum*" (I have become a debtor).

In 1967, in fact, Wojtyła had asked Father Marian Jaworski to replace him as preacher in a series of spiritual exercises. During the trip, however, there was a train crash and the priest suffered the traumatic amputation of a hand.

Jaworski was also a longtime friend, though he was six years younger. They had met in 1951, when Wojtyła was studying for his doctorate in Cracow. In 1959, after Wojtyła was made bishop, he came to live in his residence, and in 1963, when the auxiliary bishop became the archbishop of Cracow, he moved with Wojtyła into the archbishop's palace on Franciszkańska Street. What chiefly bound them together were their shared philosophical and theological interests and their involvement in the Deparment of Theology in Cracow, where Jaworski taught and was also the rector. In 1984, John Paul II named him a bishop, and in 1991 promoted him to the position of metropolitan of the Archdiocese of Lviv of the Latins, in Ukraine. After being included on an *in pectore* basis in the Consistory of 1998, in 2001 his creation as a cardinal was made public, allowing him to participate in the Conclave that on April 19, 2005, elected Benedict XVI.

Although he is nineteen years younger, there is a third Pole whose name cannot be separated from that of John

Paul II. That is, obviously, the current archbishop of Cracow, Cardinal Stanisław Dziwisz, who in 1957, during his first year of seminary, came to know Wojtyła as a professor of philosophy and, later, of moral theology and social doctrine of the Church. In 1966, the archbishop asked him to become his private secretary. In this role, Dziwisz accompanied Wojtyła to Rome for the Conclave and remained at his side for his entire papacy. In 1998, John Paul II decided to consecrate him bishop. When he objected that he was too young, Wojtyła simply pointed out that at that age he was already pope!

In the perfect inner circle, a woman has every right to be included: Dr. Wanda Półtawska, for whose recovery from a tumor Wojtyła asked and obtained the intercession of Padre Pio da Pietrelcina. The woman, a Catholic partisan fighter in Cracow, had been captured by the Nazis and confined at the Ravensbrück concentration camp, where she was subjected to inhuman medical experiments. Having survived the camp, she studied psychiatry, and met Father Karol when he was entrusted with the pastoral care of the young university students. Their acquaintance turned into a story of spiritual guidance and a close friendship, which survived intact throughout the years of the pontificate, when she and her family were frequently invited to the Vatican and to Castel Gandolfo during the summer holidays.

A letter written on October 20, 1978, just four days after his election, clearly reveals how crucial that friendship was for John Paul II: "The Lord has decided that everything we talked about on various occasions, and which to some degree you predicted after the death of Pope Paul VI, should become reality. I thank God that this time he has given me such great inner peace, which evidently was still lacking in August, and which has allowed me to live through this moment without tension. . . . In all of this, I think of you. I have always believed that you, in the concentration camp of Ravensbrück, suffered in part for me. . . . It is on the basis of this belief that I have come to the idea that yours might be my family and you a sister to me." At the bottom of the page is not the papal signature but the affectionate appellation by which Wanda often called him: "Brother."

CHOOSING HIS COLLEAGUES

Many have wondered what criteria John Paul II used to select the directors of the various offices of the Holy See and to appoint bishops in the thousands of Catholic dioceses around the world. The impression of those who knew him well is that, especially at the beginning of his pontificate, Wojtyła tended to single out personalities of elevated stature and set them like so many tiles into the mosaic of his larger pastoral project.

If it was natural to select Franciszek Macharski, who represented a clear line of continuity with his twenty-year ministry, to take his place at the helm of the archdiocese of Cracow, other appointments he made were more singular: the appointment of the then-archbishop of Munich, Joseph Ratzinger, to the leadership of the Congregation for the Doctrine of the Faith, and of the Jesuit Carlo Maria Martini, then rector of the Pontifical Gregorian University, as archbishop of Milan. These were prestigious men, selected personally by the pope without any outside consultations or suggestions.

Wojtyła considered Cardinal Ratzinger one of the most authoritative personalities within the Church and a pastor of rare virtues. He chose him, in 1981, so that he could have at his side a theologian capable of helping him to implement in concrete terms the teachings of the Second Vatican Council. "He was the ultimate theologian of the Council," as the pope so effectively described him to a friend. Their collaboration was solid and fruitful, and Wojtyła himself recognized that the theological profile of his papacy had essentially been forged in partnership with Cardinal Ratzinger.

Less straightforward was his relationship with Cardinal Martini. Wojtyła had known him since his time in Cracow, when he invited Martini to come to Poland and deliver a number of lectures on the Holy Scripture. Martini stayed in the archbishop's palace, where those events took place, and the two often spent time conversing. Still, for Martini it came as a surprise to receive, just before Christmas in 1979, an invitation to meet with the pope in the Vatican. When John Paul II, during that meeting, proposed that he become archbishop of Milan, the Jesuit revealed his concerns, explaining that, since he had always been a professor, he had no familiarity with people. Wojtyła replied, "You will not need to go to the people, the people will come to you."

The pope had been told that Martini took part in the pastoral activities of the community of Sant'Egidio, devoting himself to serving the poor as well as celebrating Mass in the poverty-stricken outskirts of Rome. Thus, to dispel the Jesuit's objections about lack of pastoral experience, he needed only to ask, "So what exactly did you used to do on Sundays with the community of Sant'Egidio?" As time went on, a number of observers had the impression that relations between them became more strained, not unlike a pair of university professors who do not agree on their analysis of the situation and the best strategy to adopt. Their mutual respect, however, never wavered.

Camillo Ruini too was chosen personally by John Paul II. At the time, Ruini was auxiliary bishop of Reggio Emilia and the pope had heard good things about him. At the beginning of 1985, he invited him to dinner at the Vatican and discussed the ecclesial situation in Italy. Finding that he and the bishop were fully in agreement, he asked Ruini to draft the speech that he would be delivering at the second Conference of the Italian Church in Loreto that April. It was probably as a result of this remarkable convergence of views that, in June 1986, Ruini was appointed secretary general of the Italian bishops' conference, and was promoted to the office of president five years later. In an appreciation of his work, John Paul II, who at the beginning of his papacy hadn't felt particularly close to the Italian bishops, stated that Cardinal Ruini "had restored the unity of the Italian episcopate with the pontiff."

With the passage of time, Pope Wojtyła relied increasingly upon the suggestions of the Secretariat of State and the Congregation for the Bishops. It was decided that, for Italy as for other countries, it would become the responsibility of the nuncio, rather than the existing special commission, to evaluate the potential candidates for vacant dioceses. So John Paul II was duly presented with a trio of names, in order of the Congregation's preference, and he generally chose the first name on the list. Yet he did not hesitate, especially when he noticed pressure being brought to bear in favor of one candidate, to opt for a name that was not on the list at all.

Despite the care he devoted to this matter of personnel, it sometimes happened that the pontiff was disappointed at the outcome of an appointment. In one case, where he probably had placed too much trust in a colleague, when someone objected to the candidate that he had selected, he replied, "I am afraid that it's too late now." Then, under his breath, as he was heading to the chapel to pray, he added, "If they lied to me, they've already lost. I'm not the leader of the Church, Jesus Christ is." And to an old friend—who had heard the detachment with which he spoke of the Curia, as if it were something that he had to work with, or around, and had said to him, "But you are the pope, you can choose who you want"—Wojtyła replied very straightforwardly, "But it's not that easy to find the right people."

A FIRMNESS UNDERPINNED
BY HUMILITY

From the very first months of his pontificate, John Paul II made clear his intention to complete the modernization of the Church in accordance with the indications of the Second Vatican Council. He involved numerous experts in a lengthy

ated the order and then put an end to the discussion with the words: "Now nothing is left to me but prayer."

The pope prayed every day not only for the bishops that he had consecrated and the priests he had ordained but also for the entire Roman Curia. He kept next to his prie-dieu a photocopy of the Vatican directory with the list of employees by name, and he had instructed his entourage to take that document to Castel Gandolfo as well. After celebrating Mass, he always included an intention for them all.

His concern for his colleagues certainly extended to those at the lower end of the hierarchy, as is evidenced by a story that one of the Swiss Guards confided to a priest. The guard had been on duty outside the papal apartments one Christmas Eve, and a number of high ecclesiastical officials had come to extend their season's greetings to the pope. "The only one who offered season's greetings to me was the pope, who came and opened the door in person to wish me 'Merry Christmas.'"

Such profound humility in his human relations was matched in his official work. In the Vatican, for instance, it is customary for an official who must issue an opinion that will then be evaluated at a higher level to add, at the end of his opinion, the abbreviation "smj," which stands for the Latin phrase *salvo meliore judicio* (provided a better judgment is not made). John Paul II had such respect for the expertise of others that he too complied with this tradition and wrote in his own hand the abbreviation "smj" at the bottom of some of the documents that he had considered and concerning which, after he had expressed his own authoritative disposition, he still wished to receive further opinions.

"IT WILL TAKE BLOOD TO CONVERT"

On Tuesday, May 12, 1981, John Paul II visited the Vatican medical center. After inspecting the facilities and meeting with the staff, he was accompanied to the exit by Dr. Renato Buzzonetti, director of the facility and his own personal physician. Pointing out a new ambulance parked nearby, the doctor asked the pope to bless it. As he sprinkled it with holy water, John Paul II said, "I also bless the first patient who will use this ambulance." Twenty-four hours later, the first patient transported in that vehicle would be none other than himself.

"If the word has not converted, then blood will convert," Cardinal Wojtyła had written, shortly before being elected to the pontificate, in the poem *Stanisław*, devoted to the martyred saint of Cracow. The assassination attempt on May 13, 1981, by Ali Ağca, would endow those verses with an evident autobiographical dimension, radically modifying the perception that the pope had of his mission. From that moment onward, his calvary began, illuminated by the awareness that he had been given life a second time, in order to be able to offer it for the benefit of all humanity. "For a man, and especially for a priest, there is nothing greater and more wonderful than this—that God sees fit to make use of him," he replied one day to a colleague who asked what he saw as the meaning of that traumatic event. He considered his shooting to have been "a grace," because, through his suffering, he had been permitted to testify to Christ and to evangelize.

In 1991, on the tenth anniversary of the attempted assassination, John Paul II traveled to Fátima to thank the Madonna. According to a witness who testified in the process of beatification, when greetings were being exchanged just before the Mass began, one of the cardinals present turned to him and said, "Holy Father, my cordial best wishes for your birthday!" The pope listened to those words and moved on, then turned on his heel and replied, "You are quite right, my first life was given to me, but then my second life was bestowed upon me ten years ago." A gift that he regularly celebrated, on the afternoon of every May 13 at the hour of the assassination attempt, by saying a Holy Mass of thanksgiving in his private chapel.

From the very beginning, the pontiff expressed the deeply held belief that it was the Virgin of Fátima who had watched over him, interceding for his life. As soon as he was strong enough, then, he asked the Polish office of the Secretariat of State to obtain for him all the books about the apparitions of the Virgin Mary to the three little shepherd children, so that he could better identify and understand the details of the story. To one friend who was able to visit him in his hospital room at the Gemelli Polyclinic on the evening of May 14, and who had said to him, "The Virgin will sustain Your Holiness in his suffering," the pope replied with great conviction, "She has watched over all of this. *Totus tuus*."

In the period immediately prior to the assassination attempt, the pontiff had begun working on a text for the celebration planned in the Basilica of Santa Maria Maggiore for

the solemn observance of Pentecost, on June 7, 1981, in commemoration of the 1,600th anniversary of the first Council
of Constantinople and the 1,550th anniversary of the Council
of Ephesus. The instructions that he subsequently gave to his
colleagues were to subdivide the speech into three acts: veneration, thanksgiving, and dedication to the Madonna. In particular, he was focused on the latter, and wished to place all of
humanity in the hands of Mary—an idea he reiterated repeatedly, on one occasion in the presence of the original statue of
the Virgin brought specially from Fátima to St. Peter's Square.

John Paul II knew that he was the potential target of a
criminal attack: "Nothing could have been easier than to
shoot at the pope, who showed himself to the people without
protection," he later commented. This awareness, however,
never led him to avoid contact with the crowd or to protect
himself in any specific way. Watching a television program
about the assassination attempt, he said calmly to a dinner
guest, "They would like it if I wore a bulletproof vest so that
I could always be secure . . . but the shepherd always has to
be in the middle of his flock, even at the cost of his own life."

Some time before the assassination attempt, the Italian
secret intelligence services had warned of a plan by the terrorist organization called the Red Brigades to kidnap John
Paul II. Perhaps that is in part why, immediately after being
shot, the pope confided to his secretary, Father Stanisław,
the instinctive thought "Just like Bachelet," with reference to
the Catholic vice president of the Italian Superior Council of
Magistrates who was assassinated in Rome by the Red Brigades on February 12, 1980.

THE POPE   91

The Holy Father also wondered about the motivations for the attempted assassination, of course, but he cared much more deeply about the spiritual interpretation of the dramatic events that he had experienced. This explains why he always preferred to assign to the Secretariat of State the task of establishing the Holy See's official position with regard to the trial of Ali Ağca, as well as pronouncing on whether or not clemency was appropriate.

To his close friends, however, he recounted having spoken about the so-called "Bulgarian connection" with the secretary of the Russian Communist Party, Mikhail Gorbachev, and with the Polish general Wojciech Jaruzelski. Gorbachev told him that he had been unable to find anything in the state archives of the USSR that supported that hypothesis, while Jaruzelski told him that at the time he had asked Todor Zhivkov, first secretary of the Bulgarian Communist Party, about it. Zhivkov had replied, "Comrade, do you think we are imbeciles? If Antonov had been involved in the assassination attempt, we would have evacuated him from Italy the following day. Instead, he remained on the job."

THE "OPEN LETTER" TO ALI AĞCA

On December 27, 1983, John Paul II had a long and intense conversation with his would-be murderer, in the Roman prison of Rebibbia. Later the pontiff declared: "Today I was able to meet my assailant and repeat to him that I forgave him, as I already did right away, as soon as I could. We met as men and as brothers and all the events of our lives bring us toward this brotherhood."

The pope had forgiven Ali Ağca immediately, communicating this to the world when he recited the "Regina Coeli," on May 17, 1981, from the Gemelli Polyclinic: "I pray for the brother who shot me, and whom I have sincerely forgiven." An attitude that, as has emerged from the testimony of several witnesses, took on an immediate emblematic significance and shook the consciences of many people. Not least among them was the Polish general Jaruzelski: after being gravely wounded in an attempted assassination in 1994, he decided not to prosecute those responsible for the attack, explaining that the pope's example had won his heart.

Previously unpublished, on the other hand, is the "open letter" that the Holy Father had begun to prepare on September 11, 1981, for the general audience on October 21 of that year. He later decided not to make that letter public, probably choosing caution in view of the ongoing investigations. The two sheets of the draft, found with a large X traced over them, read verbatim:

> 1. Today once again I would like to devote some words, during this meeting of ours in audience, to the subject of the event of May 13. On that day two men met: one who was trying to take the life of the other, and that other whose life he was trying to take. Divine Providence, however, saw to it that this life was not taken. And so that other man was able to address the first, to speak to him—this, if we consider the nature of the event, seems

particularly significant and pertinent. It is important that not even an episode like that of May 13 can succeed in opening an abyss between one man and another, cannot create a silence that signifies the breaking off of all communication. Christ—the Word incarnate—taught us words of this truth that never ceases to produce a contact between people, despite the distance that can be created by events that at times pit them one against another. Nonetheless, what I want to tell you today, my dear listeners at this audience, is intended just as much for this brother of mine who on May 13 wanted to take my life and, even though that did not happen, was still the cause of many wounds that I was forced to nurse for a number of months. Thus my words today will be in a certain sense an "open letter" (perhaps in a way similar to the letter written some time ago by Pope Paul VI after Aldo Moro was kidnapped, and yet at the same time very different).

2. The first word of this "letter"—perhaps we should say, of this open "address"—was already spoken publicly on May 17, during the Angelus [actually the "Regina Coeli"]. Allow me to quote that text (to quote all of it or at least the part that speaks of forgiveness . . . perhaps it would be best to include all of it, in remembrance as well of two people who were injured!). On Sunday May 17, these words were spoken publicly. But the possibility of pronouncing them even earlier, in the ambulance that was transporting me from the Vatican to the Gemelli Polyclinic, where the first and decisive surgery

was performed, I consider the fruit of a particular grace conceded to me by Jesus, my Lord and Teacher. Yes! I believe that it was a particular grace of the crucified Jesus who, among the words he spoke on Golgotha, first of all said that phrase "Father, forgive them; for they do not know what they are doing." The act of forgiveness is the first and fundamental condition that allows us, as humans, not to be reciprocally divided and pitted one against another, as enemies. Because we seek from God, who is our Father, understanding and union. This is important and substantial when we are talking about the behavior of one man toward another, but also . . .

The text that was actually spoken at the general audience on October 21 was in any case dedicated to the theme of forgiveness, described as "a grace and a mystery of the human heart." After remembering that "Regina Coeli" of May 17, and after quoting the passages of the Gospels in which Christ speaks of forgiveness, Pope Wojtyła continued: "At that time, then, when the man who tried to take my life was being tried and when he was given his sentence, I thought about the story of Cain and Abel, which biblically expresses the 'beginning' of the sin against human life. In our times, when that sin has become again, and in a new manner, threatening, while so many innocent men perish at the hands of other men, the biblical description of what happened between Cain and Abel becomes particularly eloquent. Even more complete, even more disturbing than the very commandment 'Thou shalt not kill.'"

And he concluded: "Christ taught us to forgive. Forgiveness is indispensable also so that God can pose questions to the human conscience, expecting answers in all our inner truth. In these days, when so many innocent men perish at the hands of other men, it would appear that we are under a special imperative to approach each of those who kill, approach them with forgiveness in our hearts and at the same time, with the same question that God, Creator and Lord of human life, asked the first man who tried to take the life of his brother, and indeed took it—took what is the property only of the Creator and Lord of life. Christ taught us to forgive. He taught Peter to forgive "seventy-seven times" (Matthew 18:22). God himself forgives when man answers the question addressed to his conscience and to his heart with all the inner truth of conversion. Leaving to God himself the judgment and the sentence in its definitive dimension, we cannot stop asking: 'Forgive us our debts, as we also have forgiven our debtors.'"

"OPEN THE BORDERS OF THE STATES"

For the Polish authorities, the year 1981 was an *annus horribilis*, because the attempted assassination of the pontiff on May 13 and the death of the primate Stefan Wyszyński on May 28 both coincided with a phase of high tension in the domestic political and social domain. This inevitably had serious repercussions on relations between the Warsaw regime and the Soviet Union.

The unrest guided by Solidarity, the labor union founded the previous August to protest against the economic crisis in Poland and to demand greater workers' rights, had aroused serious concerns among the Soviet leaders. They, in turn, ordered the Polish authorities to put an end to the wave of strikes or risk direct intervention by the Red Army.

The spring and summer of 1981 saw a succession of increasingly frantic meetings of the Polish Communist Party's top leaders, summoned to decide the next moves. Jaruzelski, who in that state of emergency had assumed the dual role of head of state and party secretary, clearly understood that, whatever strategy he chose to adopt, one of his severest judges would be John Paul II, who, from his very first visit to Poland in June 1979, had sent an unmistakable message that he would never abandon the land of his birth to its fate.

One authoritative Polish politician recalled the strong impression it had made upon him when, during that visit, he heard John Paul II state that perhaps the election of a Slavic pope was a sign that East and West could come to an understanding. When he later met him in the 1990s, this politician remarked, "Holy Father, those words sounded like a prophecy," and the pope replied, "You remember very well. Primate Wyszyński read those words in advance, and he said: 'Oh, Lolek, use caution, use caution!'" But the pope was convinced that it was time to venture an extra step forward, however great the risks.

In the fall, the Polish authorities understood that a direct confrontation with John Paul II was now unavoidable. On October 13, 1981, therefore, the Polish foreign minister Józef

Czyrek arrived at the Apostolic Palace to lay out the seriousness of the situation and the potential paths forward. The
pope was still very weak in the aftermath of the assassination attempt, but he listened with great interest to the Polish envoy and made arrangements for the new primate, Józef
Glemp, and the labor leader, Lech Wałęsa, to meet General
Jaruzelski. That meeting took place on November 4, and the
following day Archbishop Glemp came to the papal apartments to report the results of that meeting, which seemed to
offer some promise.

In the weeks that followed, however, Soviet pressure for a
rapid solution to the crisis, which was threatening to spread
to other East Bloc countries, caused a sharp worsening of the
situation. On the night of December 13, martial law was proclaimed in Poland. A few days later, the Vatican nuncio, Luigi
Poggi, arrived in Warsaw, bringing a fairly sternly worded letter from the Holy Father.

A rapid negotiation with the party directors, Kazimierz
Barcikowski and Jerzy Kuberski, resulted in a softening of the
tone. In any case, in the official letter John Paul II expressed
his great distress at the proclamation of martial law, appeal-
ing at the same time that it be revoked as soon as possible
and a path to dialogue be rapidly found. The response from
the general, sent on January 6, 1982, also took the most con-
ciliatory of tones, while clearly laying out the factors that had
driven him to make that decision.

The pontiff always maintained a dialogue on a personal
level with Jaruzelski. It was in fact during a private conversation at the Wawel Cathedral in June 1983 that the general

first made known to John Paul II his intention of abolishing once and for all martial law and undertaking a series of reforms. The pope's reply was: "I understand that socialism is a reality, but let's try to do whatever we can to give it a human face. Civil liberties, social identity, and human rights are all important." Jaruzelski saw this observation as an encouragement to lead Poland, step-by-step, toward a different form of politics. "He neither scolded nor offered warnings," the general recalled, "but instead took into consideration the problems of the moment, indicating what he felt was the best course for the country."

This was Wojtyła's usual approach to confrontations, as is confirmed by the testimony of, among others, a person who, discussing with him a series of historical occurrences, noted that Providence sometimes makes use of the worst events to do good. The pontiff replied with these words: "Maybe you are right. But keep in mind that it is not enough to be right, the problem is how to convince people to accept this truth."

In Poland, a gradual transition to democracy thus became possible, a transition that had to some degree begun the instant news arrived of Karol Wojtyła's election to the pontificate. His carefully constructed speech, with the famous appeal "Be not afraid! Open up; no: swing wide the gates to Christ. Open up to his saving power the confines of the state, open up economic and political systems, the vast empires of culture, civilization, and development," actually did produce the first cracks in the dike of Communism.

Before that, a young Polish priest recounts, "we were aware of the abnormality of the social situation in which we were living: the elections were a farce, politics was a big lie. Yet it seemed like a world that was destined to endure forever. No one could imagine that one day there would be no more state socialism in Poland and that we would be able to simply say no to the *diktats* of Moscow. On that sixteenth of October 1978, on the other hand, it seemed that our world could be moving in a different direction, because it was no longer condemned to remain trapped in the mechanism that was driving us to desperation and meaninglessness."

Communism buried the individual in the masses, but paradoxically it was afraid of the masses. It wanted the masses to remain stupid and unaware of the power they possessed. For that reason, during the period of martial law, police authorization was required even to hold a party at home for a birthday or a name day if there were more than a certain number of guests. Little by little, however, people began looking around and losing their fear, realizing how many other people shared their values. And credit for this can certainly be attributed in part to Pope Wojtyła.

THE COLLAPSE OF COMMUNISM

If the collapse of Communism, from 1989 on, took place without the terrible bloodshed that could easily have accompanied it, this too was in part due to the efforts of John Paul II, his firm and heartfelt public appeals and the behind-the-scenes diplomacy that he encouraged. As one well-connected and experienced political figure testified, "Everyone provided a contribution—the United States' Ronald Reagan, Britain's Margaret Thatcher, France's François Mitterrand—but the Holy Father was needed to tie it all together. He never prodded anyone, never made any proposals, never schemed. He provided words, and these were sufficient." Even the Russian premier Mikhail Gorbachev acknowledged this when he said, "I did not destroy Communism, John Paul II did."

The pope and Gorbachev spoke in person for the first time on December 1, 1989, in the Vatican, and their meeting was sealed with a long handshake. The Soviet premier had been given some advice by Jaruzelski, among others. When Gorbachev and Jaruzelski met again, the Soviet leader said, "You were right. The pope is a great man. He has great wisdom and great goodness. We must do what we can to improve relations between the Soviet Union and the Vatican."

In 1992, Gorbachev sent the Vatican a two-page memo in Cyrillic titled *On the Pope of Rome*, in which he confirmed his belief that the pontiff had played a decisive role in this major historical shift. John Paul II's comment was: "I read Gorbachev's opinion on the role of the pope in the events that changed Eastern Europe in the past few years. I am convinced that he sincerely believes these things. When the European Synod of Bishops issued their final document, they wanted to emphasize this specific role of the pope, but I asked them not to. It was the Church that counted in this process, not the pope. If anything can be attributed to the pope, it's the fruit of his faithfulness: faithfulness to Christ and to mankind."

For Pope Wojtyła, everything had to be considered from the viewpoint of faith. When Communism was still powerful, he would have long discussions with intellectual friends about the way things would turn out. His conclusion was very simple: if Communism collapsed tomorrow morning, the Church's first job would be to evangelize; and if Communism collapsed in a thousand years, it would still be to evangelize. "Nothing happens by chance, all is decided from on high," he often said, quoting a German proverb, to indicate that Divine Providence guides human life down to the minor details, and that the attitude of men should be trustful, placing themselves in the hands of God, not rejecting or inwardly rebelling.

An anecdote in that connection dates from the planning period for the trip to Poland in June 1997. In the November 1995 elections, Wałęsa had been defeated by Kwaśniewski, leader of the Democratic Left Alliance, and John Paul II was wondering, a bit nervously, how he would be welcomed by the Polish people. One evening, while they were discussing this at dinner, a priest said to him, with a certain naïveté, "Holy Father, perhaps we should consider this matter in the light of Providence." The pope looked at him wryly, winked, and replied with a smile, "I do know a little something about Divine Providence!"

Pope Wojtyła was well aware that Providence intervenes where man allows God the space to enter, where man renders himself willing to reciprocate with his own actions the gifts received. He did not propose himself—nor did he perceive himself—as a protagonist, but merely as a simple tool in the hands of God. When he was told that, thanks to his prayers, someone had obtained what was requested, he commented humbly, "Thanks be to God for their faith." Likewise, when he was thanked for having contributed to the collapse of the Berlin Wall, he replied, "It was the Providence of God. The one who did it all was the Madonna," certain of the prophecy of the Virgin of Fátima concerning the conversion of Russia and the ensuing collapse of Communism. To those who asked him whether it was easy to experience history in the first person, he replied, "When God wishes it, it becomes easy. This makes my life much simpler: we know that God wishes it. He arranges matters."

There can be no doubt that John Paul II had a powerful influence on the history of the twentieth century, but he did so above all by insisting on the central role of the human being, and defending the value of the individual. This insistence on the dignity of each person offered an invaluable element of cohesion that made possible, for instance, the "velvet revolution" in Czechoslovakia and the emergence in Poland of the Solidarity movement, which included believers and nonbelievers. And all of them found in the Church the space of liberty.

THE HEIR TO ST. PAUL

In the mid-1990s, a joke circulated in the Vatican: "What is the difference between God and John Paul II? God is in all places, but the pope has already been there." Wojtyła knew that the decision to devote so much energy to his pastoral travels in Italy and abroad met with a degree of disapproval.

He attempted to counter that disapproval as early as June 1980 by stating publicly: "Many say that the pope travels too much, and too often. I think that, in human terms, they are right. But it is Providence that guides us, and sometimes it suggests that we do something *per excessum*."

Indeed, during the pontificate of Pope Wojtyła, statistics entered the hushed halls of the Vatican with a vengeance. The apostolic journeys that he made were 146 in Italy and 104 abroad, in a sequence that included no fewer than 259 Italian localities and 131 independent nations. The number of days he spent away from the Vatican, without counting his stays at the summer residence of Castel Gandolfo and the 164 days he spent in the hospital, reached the impressive number of 822, equivalent to 8.5 percent of his entire pontificate.

John Paul II considered himself not only the successor to St. Peter but also the heir to St. Paul "who, as we know very well, never stayed long in one place: he was always traveling." In this there was an element of continuity with the papacy of Pope Paul VI, who had begun a significant, albeit brief, sequence of apostolic journeys in the context of the opening and decentralization of the Church as recommended by the Second Vatican Council. John Paul II, for his part, said, "I am traveling as a teacher of faith, but also as a disciple, to learn about the life of the local churches."

Certainly the papal trips demanded an investment of resources that was often staggering—and that often prompted objections and criticism, which profoundly grieved John Paul II. During his pastoral visitation to Australia, for instance, a number of local newspapers attacked him, pointing out that his trip had cost more than an earlier trip by the Queen of England. Whereupon the pope, speaking to a member of the entourage, replied with great firmness, "I believe that the trips of the pope should in fact cost more than those of the Queen of England: the pope brings the message of redemption, and redemption had an incalculable cost, that is all of Christ's blood."

Besides, these travels allowed millions of people who could never have afforded to travel to the Vatican to see the pontiff in person and to hear his words. "If the world cannot come to Rome, Rome must go out to the world," Wojtyła announced in a vivid turn of phrase to the Peruvian bishops.

It often happened as well that a visit by the pope served to focus attention on the humanitarian emergencies of countries in difficulty, or to give a voice to oppressed populations. The pope also tended to contribute to those recipients all the donations that had been collected around the time of the voyage. Above all, however, he was aware that his job was to spread everywhere the hope of the Gospels. In a very poor area outside Lima, Peru, at the end of his sermon, he looked out at the multitude of people crowding the space and, improvising, he uttered in Spanish an idea that surged up from the bottom of his heart, "Hunger for God, yes; hunger for bread, no." And on another occasion, as he recited the Lord's Prayer, he affirmed, "I want there to be people who hunger after God, not people who hunger after their daily bread."

Every trip was planned with dedication and concentration. John Paul II asked his nuncios to assemble the national bishops' conference to ask what the bishops and their clergy wanted, established direct contacts with the pastors of the places where he would be traveling to obtain all possible useful information, read everything that was available, and absorbed a vast quantity of details by talking to experts.

For several weeks prior to his departure, he celebrated Mass in the language that he would be using in the country to which he would travel, usually with the participation of priests and nuns from the place in question. In that way, he wished to pay tribute to the culture of each people, as well as to sacralize their language through the celebration of the liturgy. He kept dictionaries and specific handbooks on his desk, consulting them from time to time, and relying upon native-speaking Vatican employees to refine his pronunciation.

Before going to Mexico, for instance, for many weeks he spent an hour every morning improving his Spanish. When he was preparing for his voyage to Papua New Guinea, he relied upon two Divine Word missionaries to teach him enough pidgin to pronounce a few phrases of greeting to the indigenous people. Before going to Japan, he studied with a Japanese Franciscan the pronunciation of that language and had him transcribe the speeches phonetically. And when he went to Guam, he listened to hours of recordings of greetings in Chamorro, the local indigenous language.

With his Roman colleagues, he debated at length about the draft plan for the journey. Generally the number of appointments proposed by the local churches was so great that it became necessary to extend the length of the trip by a day or two, and the pope nearly always agreed readily. In any case, he never failed to meet with the priests, the male and female religious, the seminarians and the novices of the male and female congregations, and especially the young people and the sick.

John Paul II certainly took a particular interest in this last category, and not only because he himself had experienced infirmity. During the first trip abroad, the one in 1979 to Mexico, he found himself in a church full of the infirm, the handicapped, and invalids. As one of his travel companions recalled, "The pope stopped at each patient and I had the distinct impression that he stood in veneration before each of them: he leaned toward them, did his best to understand what they were saying, and then caressed their heads." The master of ceremonies soon realized that, for the Masses to be celebrated by the pope during his pastoral missions around the world, they should never put more than thirty sick people facing the altar. Otherwise, since John Paul II would always greet them one by one at the end of the service, there would be a run-on delay and he would miss all the other events.

In one instance where this consideration was not taken into account, a first group of sick people was placed across from the security barriers, and immediately behind them another group of about three hundred was positioned, many of them in wheelchairs. The pontiff summoned the coordinator and ordered an opening to be made so that he could pass through and greet them all: that day, the program was delayed by almost an hour. Another time, when he visited a hospital ward, he stopped to greet every patient. The prefect of the papal household, Monsignor Dino Monduzzi, suggested he pick up the pace, but Wojtyła not only ignored the suggestion but also scolded him: "Monsignor, with those who are suffering you must never be in a hurry."

IN THE WORLD'S "HOT ZONES"

From the very earliest days, John Paul II made clear to his colleagues what the style of his pontificate would be. He gave a clear example when he answered affirmatively the proposal of the Latin American episcopate that he take part in the Puebla Conference, which was scheduled to take place in Mexico in January 1979. The Roman Curia was opposed to the journey, and laid out the risks to which the pontiff would be exposed, in a nation where religious faith could not be manifested in public. After hearing the various opinions, Wojtyła swept away all objections: "I don't have a Secretariat of State to tell me what the problems are, but to solve them." The pastoral visitation took place and it was a spectacular success.

Less straightforward was the 1987 trip to Chile, which had been under the dictatorship of Augusto Pinochet since 1973. John Paul II placed a condition, a sine qua non, that he should be able to meet one and all, including groups in political opposition to the regime. One episode occurred, however, that cast a shadow over the entire visit. This was when, from the presidential palace in Santiago, the pope and Pinochet appeared side by side to salute the cheering crowd. Eyewitnesses affirm that the appearance was not part of the program and was a "trick" staged by the dictator. What happened was that Pinochet led Wojtyła down a corridor from which the people outside could be seen and, unexpectedly, invited the pope to look out the window and bless the faithful. The pope did not refuse, but in their private conversation he also did not refrain from telling the dictator what he felt was appropriate.

History has shown the effect that this conversation had on subsequent events. Not long afterward, the pope told a friend, "I received a letter from Pinochet in which he told me that, as a Catholic, he had listened to my words, he had accepted them, and he had decided to begin the process to change the leadership of his country." And in fact the elections promised for 1988 did take place: Pinochet was forced to accept his defeat and, in 1990, gave up the office of president. Commenting on this episode, Wojtyła observed that it was necessary to meet everyone, without exception, but to do so with the simplicity and strength that derive from the Gospels.

The trip to Nicaragua, in March 1983, was probably the one most freighted with risk. At the time, the Communist movement of the Sandinistas held power, and a part of the clergy, in the context of the doctrine of liberation theology, had joined ranks with the revolutionaries in favor of a popular church, opposed to the hierarchical church. Presented with the attendant difficulties, John Paul II was certain: "We must go, even though it will not be a great success. This church needs to be reinforced now, when it is passing through a very critical moment. Then we can hope that better times will come, and that the pope will receive a better welcome, but I must go there now as well."

The people in charge of Vatican security, after performing a preliminary inspection, determined that there was a grave threat to the lives of the Holy Father and the people traveling with him. They therefore decided that everyone would have to wear bulletproof vests under their cassocks. When John Paul II was informed of this recommendation, he said only, "If any in my entourage wish to wear a bulletproof vest, they need not accompany me on this visit. We are in the hands of God and we will be protected by him." On another occasion, with the subtle irony that distinguished him, the pope offered this reply to the French cardinal Albert Decourtray, who had reminded him of the dire prophecy of Nostradamus concerning his journey to Lyons in 1986: "I assure you, Your Eminence, that no place is as dangerous as St. Peter's Square!"

Incidentally many who knew him were struck by the way his sense of humor never failed him. Once, after making a difficult decision, he commented, "We are in the hands of God . . . and it's a good thing, because if we were in our hands, we would already be lost." During an exchange of gifts, as he extended to a political leader a painting of St. Peter's Square, he explained, "St. Peter's Square. How shall I say? It's where I work!" And when a journalist asked him if he felt he was in good shape for the upcoming 1998 voyage to Cuba, he responded, "Certainly I am older than I was in 1979, but so far Providence has preserved me. And then, if I want to know anything about my health and my infirmities, I can read about it in the press!"

With reference to his travels in Latin America, certain critics accused him of employing a double standard, showing greater indulgence toward right-wing dictatorships than toward their left-wing counterparts. To this provocation John Paul II responded with an explanation based on his own personal experience: "A right-wing dictatorship is the dictatorship of a single man, and when that man dies, the regime dies with him. A left-wing dictatorship, in contrast, is guided by a system, and that is much more difficult to uproot." Behind what some interpreted as a compromise with power, there was actually a desire to emphasize the spirit of reconciliation rather than opposition, and to somehow encourage a peaceful transition to democracy.

Without doubt, however, there were those in his entourage who showed a greater inclination to the right than to the left. One such instance was the initial omission from the Ecumenical Commemoration of Witnesses to the Faith in the Twentieth Century held on May 7, 2000, in the Colosseum, of the name of Monsignor Oscar Romero, the archbishop of San Salvador who was murdered in 1980 while he was celebrating Mass. When that absence was mentioned to him, Pope Wojtyła justified it by explaining that a collaborator had described Romero to him as a "banner of the left." But then he examined the question more closely and ordered that Romero be included. For that matter, during the planning of the 1983 pastoral voyage to El Salvador, when someone suggested that he not visit the archbishop's grave, he replied in no uncertain terms, "No, the pope must go, this was a bishop who was murdered in the very midst of his pastoral ministry, during the celebration of the Holy Mass."

The pontiff never shirked a difficult decision. In 1982, a visit to Great Britain was already planned, from May 28 to June 2, when war broke out with Argentina over the possession of the Malvinas, or Falkland Islands. It was suggested that he postpone the trip, but he decided instead to add another trip, ten days later, to Argentina—twenty-nine hours of travel and only a twenty-eight-hour stay—to send a signal that war could not hinder the pope from performing his ministry among the peoples of the world. He showed the same determination three years later on the occasion of a planned visit to the Netherlands. The Dutch church at the time was riven by bitter internal disputes, and the Secretariat of State recommended waiting for better times, but John Paul II retorted that the crisis made the trip, if anything, even more necessary, an opportunity to begin a concrete program of reconstruction.

In particularly delicate situations, he did not hesitate to bypass the official institutional channels in favor of unconventional ones. This happened, for instance, when he expressed the intention to travel, in a single journey, to the three principal ethnic entities in the Balkans: the Croatian capital of Zagreb, the Bosnian capital of Sarajevo, and the Serbian capital of Belgrade. Unbeknownst to the Secretariat of State, he asked a trusted bishop to establish secret contacts to determine the feasibility of the plan. It seemed to meet with the favor of the various political leaders—Franjo Tudjman, Radovan Karadžić, Alija Izetbegović, and Slobodan Milošević—but not that of Patriarch Pavle of the Serbian Orthodox Church. When someone from the Secretariat of

State expressed disappointment at this unusual method of doing business, the pope replied with serenity, "In the Secretariat of State there is a First Section, there is a Second Section, and there can also be another section. . . . There's no reason to be shocked, we just need to get to the objective, and sometimes unofficial channels can get us there. In time, it will become clear."

John Paul II experienced with extraordinary sensitivity the pain of the victims of natural calamities, and never hesitated to travel to bring comfort in person to the stricken populations. He did this on November 25, 1980, when he chose to go to the earthquake-devastated Italian regions of Campania and Basilicata, and again six years later when he went to Colombia in July 1986 to visit the territory that had been engulfed a few months earlier by the eruption of the volcano of Nevado del Ruiz. He descended from the helicopter that had brought him to the sands of that immense tomb, fell to his knees, and prayed at length in silence, visibly moved. On his return, he reflected, "Humanity, crushed! But humanity cannot be crushed, because God was crushed in Christ. This is difficult to comprehend: God crushed! Not even Peter could understand it."

The *mysterium iniquitatis* (the "mystery of iniquity" that is mentioned in the second Epistle of Paul to the Thessalonians) constituted one of the chief points of reflection for the pontiff. John Paul II referred explicitly to it as he looked with sadness at the images of the terrorist attacks on the Twin Towers in New York. Even in those dramatic moments, however, his gaze of faith managed to win out over all emotions. As a privileged witness recounted, "In the very instant in which he had a presentiment of the apocalypse, on September 11, 2001, the pope turned to him who is the source of all grace, saying to him: 'They are yours.' It was an act of total trust. It was the most difficult act: it was as if he were reminding God himself of his duty. It was one of those moments of struggle with God in order to concede his grace. It belongs among the greatest moments in the history of spirituality. Like Moses. However, unlike Moses, John Paul II never chose to turn away from his own people."

A MATCHLESS MAGISTERIUM

During an international voyage, a journalist asked Pope Wojtyła whether he felt he was too critical in his speeches. His reply was, "I have thought about that sometimes, but I have always seen that the word of God is much more demanding, and my duty is to proclaim it at all times."

There can be no doubt that John Paul II fully performed this duty, not only by addressing the world with a stupefying quantity of speeches and documents, but also by conveying his message always in language that was clear and accessible to all.

From the very first days of his pontificate, he began to reflect on the question of how he should present the customary catechesis during the general audience on Wednesdays. He had asked a number of specialists to help him gather material on specific themes, identifying the biblical passages and doctrinal sections from the Church Fathers that seemed best to explore. Then, however, he considered the best way to write the texts, to ensure that they were comprehensible to the greatest possible number of listeners. "I have learned how to write in poetic language, philosophical language, and homiletic language, but I'm not really sure what it means to speak in catechetic language. Yet I realize that the way in which the message is transmitted also determines the acceptance of the content," he confided to his closest collaborators. With those who assisted him in composing the texts, he was very demanding: he always wanted to put his mark on the texts, both in terms of content and in terms of form.

During a luncheon at Castel Gandolfo, he said, referring to himself, "I don't know whether history will remember this pope; I doubt it. If so, I hope that he will be remembered as the pope of the family." In fact, issues linked to marriage and the family were always at the heart of his pastoral concerns. When speaking with people who were divorced or remarried, he was never judgmental or accusatory. Quite the opposite. "What struck me deeply," one authoritative witness recalled, "were his expressions of affection and love toward people who are struggling with a difficult family situation. I felt all the afflatus of forgiveness and reconciliation that so often may not be perceived in the same way on those public occasions when the Church and its teachings are expressed on these matters."

Unquestionably, his pastoral commitment to the laity was just as great. He considered the ecclesial movements authentic "signs of the times," and he valued and appreciated all initiatives that were aimed at announcing the message of the Gospels, on the biblical principle that if something is created by men, it will die, but if it comes from God, we must not oppose it but rather comply with it, because it may well be a gift of Providence. In the pontiff's view, however, it was appropriate to ensure that the new lay organizations not be confused with the religious structures, and on more than one occasion he opposed the request of those who wished to transform themselves into a secular institute under the umbrella of the Congregation for Institutes of Consecrated Life and Societies of Apostolic Life (formerly Congregation for Religious and Secular Institutes), suggesting instead that they try for recognition from the Pontifical Council for the Laity.

Pope Wojtyła was absolutely certain that the laity was destined to acquire greater power and prominence within the Church. It was this awareness that impelled him to institute World Youth Days, beginning with the historic event in Rome in the square in front of the Basilica of St. John Lateran in March 1985. The United Nations had proclaimed that year the International Year of Youth, and John Paul II decided to celebrate with a massive gathering. A number of his colleagues doubted that the initiative could succeed, but the pope was confident: "We must make a beginning, for this is the future of the Church." The success of the event was spectacular, and from that day forward, Palm Sunday was devoted to this mass gathering.

The huge initiative in Rome also represented, in a certain sense, an opportunity to translate into reality another of John Paul II's heartfelt aspirations: to make his diocese an example for the rest of the Catholic world. How could he exhort the other bishops to make their dioceses vibrant, he often said to the cardinal vicar and to the auxiliary bishops, if his own diocese did not lead the way? Playing on the *Roma/amor* palindrome in Latin, he summarized the ecclesial mandate with the emblematic words "La missione di *Roma* è *amor*" (The mission of Rome is love), thereby placing special emphasis on his role as the bishop of Rome and on the Roman tradition of *Urbi et Orbi*—*urbi* referring to Rome and *orbi* to the world at large, the two forming a single pastoral strategy. He had had a large map of the diocese of Rome hung on one of his bedroom walls, with all of the parishes identified. Many, clearly marked over the course of the years, had already been visited; many others, as he himself was forced to acknowledge from time to time when he stopped to examine the map, were still waiting.

He also felt a great pastoral responsibility toward Italy. "As the bishop of this apostolic see and as the primate of Italy, I feel that I am a participant in the destiny, in the joys and the sufferings, of all the people of Italy," he clearly stated. It was he who encouraged, in 1994, the initiative of the prayer for Italy, that the severe crisis afflicting the country might be serenely overcome. On January 6 of that year, he even sent a personal letter to the Italian bishops, with a serious reminder of the responsibilities that Catholics were obliged to assume in the face of the challenges of that historical moment.

John Paul II was especially concerned about the secessionist divides that threatened Italy's national unity. As an eyewitness from that period recalled, "I still remember clearly the pope's concern during the summer of 1996, when the

Northern League staged a gathering at the source of the Po River. He perceived their political gesture as a crime against Italian unity, and he asked me why the Italian carabinieri did not intervene, and why the president of the Italian Republic was doing nothing. He was well aware what a precious resource Italy constituted for the Holy See and for the pope. This conviction was a major factor as well in his decision to add to the responsibilities of the cardinal vicar of Rome the role of president of the Italian bishops' conference."

IN DIALOGUE WITH THE OTHER FAITHS

A man of dialogue and engagement, John Paul II did not hesitate to work to orient his papacy toward the achievement of an ambitious ecumenical project. That undertaking had one of its most intensely emblematic moments in the interreligious meeting that took place in Assisi on October 27, 1986, the World Day of Prayer for Peace.

Knowing full well that the idea could lead to mixed messages and missed signals, the pope reflected at length before announcing it publicly. Then, encouraged by the support of then-cardinal Joseph Ratzinger, who had expressed a positive opinion at lunch, he decided to announce the event personally during the general audience of October 22, explaining that the World Day of Prayer for Peace would be an opportunity "to gather together and pray . . . side by side, to implore God to give the gift that all humanity now needs more than any other in order to survive: peace."

While remaining firmly convinced that Jesus Christ was the sole Savior of the world, John Paul II still held in his heart the possibility of a dialogue with other religious faiths in which, in accordance with the teachings of the Second Vatican Council, he encountered the presence of "rays of the one truth." Indeed, according to one witness, "the fruit of Assisi was that, instead of hostility and enmity between religions, the principle of a dialogue was introduced." For this reason as well, the pontiff, despite the disagreement of some cardinals who saw the World Day of Prayer for Peace in Assisi as a one-time thing, insisted that the experience be reprised each year, in a different town in Europe or the Mediterranean basin, and made the community of Sant'Egidio responsible for the event.

Wojtyła evinced an attitude of remarkable openness and flexibility toward the Islamic world, and consistently reiterated this position. While speaking with a major political figure about the idea of Turkey entering the European Union, he observed, "If we had to judge from history, we might not expect much good to come of this, but we must look to the future and the need to prevent the triumph of selfishness and fanaticism of religious origin."

This enlightened propensity for dialogue received its emblematic seal on May 14, 1999, when Raphael I Bidawid, the Iraqi Chaldean patriarch, was received in the Vatican, accompanied by a number of civil and religious authorities from Iraq. At the end of the audience, some Muslim members of the delegation presented a copy of the Koran as a gift to the pontiff. He bowed and kissed the book in a sign of respect.

Interpreting this extraordinary gesture as a doctrinal concession on the part of the pontiff, many attacked him with malicious criticisms and insinuations. In truth, that kiss was nothing more than an instrument through which a man of faith expressed his profound charity toward the people and culture that acknowledge Abraham as the common father of all those who believe in one God. In its directness and simplicity, moreover, that gesture appealed to the sensibilities of his interlocutors, communicating an implicit yet unequivocal appeal for reciprocity.

This was not the only time that an action intended by the pontiff to revitalize relations with another confession was clearly misinterpreted. On June 29, 1995, the pope welcomed to St. Peter's Basilica the patriarch of Constantinople, Bartholomew I, and recited with him the Creed in its Constantinopolitan form, thereby limiting himself to stating that the Holy Spirit "proceeds from the Father" without the addition of "and from the Son" (*Filioque*). It is an exquisitely theological topic, but for centuries it has divided the Eastern and Western churches.

Of course, behind his decision was not a generic subscription to a vague and abstract "let's all just love one another," but rather the determination to accelerate the process of communion between sister churches, in the desire, as he explained in the sermon from that day, to "dissipate a misunderstanding that still casts a shadow on relations between Catholics and Orthodox." In fact, that meeting led to the establishment of a mixed commission with "the duty to explain, in the light of their shared faith, the legitimate significance and the legitimate scope of differing traditional expressions concerning the eternal origin of the Holy Spirit in the Trinity, expressions that belong to our reciprocal doctrinal and liturgical heritages."

The fear on the part of the Orthodox that the Church of Rome might harbor ambitions to proselytize among their faithful proved entirely unfounded. The pope, especially during the time he was working on the encyclical *Ut unum sint*, in which he opened to discussion even the exercise of the Petrine supremacy, often repeated, as if it were a slogan: "With the Orthodox, what I want is communion, not jurisdiction."

And in his quest to experience common gestures of communion and prayer, he did not hesitate to make use of minor subterfuges, such as the "trick" he played on the Orthodox bishop of Athens in the Vatican nunciature in Greece. During their brief, informal meeting, Wojtyła said to the bishop at a certain point that he would like to recite the Lord's Prayer in the Greek language. Caught by surprise, the Greek religious authorities began reciting the Lord's Prayer in their own language and the pope accompanied them, also in Greek.

One problematic issue, explored during the cause for beatification, was the Eucharistic Communion that John Paul II personally imparted on more than one occasion to Frère (Brother) Roger Schutz, the founder of the ecumenical community of Taizé, who was stabbed to death by a schizophrenic woman on August 16, 2005. Since Schutz was not formally a Catholic, but rather a Protestant, this was not technically legitimate. In reality, as Monsignor Gérard Daucourt, bishop of Nanterre, declared, "Frère Roger had converted to Catholicism and the pope, along with the bishops of Autun, knew that, even though they had not said anything about it publicly." Others too have testified that, in spite of the absence of any formal transition to the Catholic Church from the ecclesial community in which Frère Roger had been baptized, there can be no doubt about his completely genuine faith in the real presence of Christ in the Eucharist.

Wojtyła and Frère Roger had first met during the Second Vatican Council, when Wojtyła was vicar capitular. Every morning when he went to the Basilica of St. Peter to pray in the presence of the Most Holy Sacrament, he would encounter Frère Roger in the chapel. Later, in 1964 and in 1968, Archbishop Wojtyła traveled to Taizé, knowing that Frère Roger, without breaking with his origins, had adhered in his heart to the Catholic faith. The first time that Wojtyła gave Communion to Frère Roger was in May 1973, when he was cardinal and Frère Roger was his guest in Cracow and they met with two hundred thousand Polish miners during the pilgrimage to Katowice. On that occasion, Frère Roger personally informed him that he had been admitted to the Eucharist by his bishop of Autun, Monsignor Armand-François Le Bourgeois, since September 1972.

"THERE IS NO PLACE IN THE CHURCH FOR A POPE EMERITUS"

As Pope Wojtyła grew older, he began to consider whether it might not be appropriate to submit his resignation in a situation in which he was manifestly incapable of performing his ministry. By now nearly seventy-five years old (that birthday would come on May 18, 1995), he undertook an informal consultation with the directors of the Secretariat of State and with his closest friends and colleagues, discussing with them as well whether it was right to apply to himself the regulation of Canon Law that calls for bishops to leave office when they turn seventy-five. The deterioration of his physical condition led him to take this possibility very seriously, although he was well aware of the problems that the presence of a pope emeritus could potentially entail.

He therefore had the subject studied from both a historical and a theological point of view, consulting in particular with then-cardinal Ratzinger, prefect of the Congregation for the Doctrine of the Faith. In the end, however, he put the decision in the hands of God. In substance, he did nothing more than confirm what he had already said in 1994 to the surgeon Gianfranco Fineschi, who had just operated on him for a fractured femur: "Doctor, both you and I have only one choice. You must heal me. And I must heal. Because there is no place in the Church for a pope emeritus." The decision not to leave the throne of Peter found its roots in the spirituality of abandonment of self to God and in the faith in Divine Providence and in the trusty assistance of the Madonna. Summarizing its most essential passages, his mental process might have run something like this: I never expected to become pope. Divine Providence brought me to this point. Now it is not up to me to put an end to this task. The Lord has brought me here; I will leave it up to him to judge and decide when this service of mine should end. If I were to renounce the pontificate, I would be making that decision, but I want to perform in full the will of God: I leave the decision to him.

This is what the pontiff wrote in a text dating from 1994, and probably meant to be read aloud (to the College of Cardinals?), since on several of the words the accent was marked in pen to aid him in the pronunciation:

> Before God, I have reflected at length about what the pope should do for himself when he turns seventy-five. In this connection, I will confide to you that when, two years ago, the possibility arose that a tumor that had to be operated on might prove malignant, I thought that the Father who is in heaven might have decided to solve the problem a little early. But that is not the way it went.
>
> After praying and meditating at length on my responsibilities before God, I believe that it is my duty to follow the provisions and example of Pope Paul VI, who, when the same problem arose, judged that he could renounce the apostolic mandate only in the presence of an incurable illness or an impediment that would prevent him from performing the functions of Successor to Peter.
>
> Therefore, I too, following in the footsteps of my Predecessor, had already put in writing my intention to renounce the sacred and canonical office of Roman Pontiff in the case of an infirmity that is judged to be incurable and that prevents me from exercising [adequately] the duties of the Petrine ministry.
>
> This eventuality aside, I see as a grave obligation in my conscience the duty to continue to perform the

duties to which Christ Our Lord has summoned me, for as long as he, in the mysterious designs of his Providence, shall wish.

The text by Pope Paul VI to which Pope Wojtyła refers was dated February 2, 1965, and was also cited in Pope Wojtyła's earlier unpublished manuscript (the "already put in writing" document) dated February 15, 1989, which reads:

Following the example of the Holy Father Paul VI (see the text dated February 2, 1965) I declare:

—in the case of a long-term infirmity that is judged to be incurable, and that prevents me from exercising adequately the duties of my apostolic ministry,

—or else in the case that another grave and prolonged impediment prove to be an equivalent obstacle,

—that I will renounce my sacred and canonical office, both as bishop of Rome and as head of the Holy Catholic Church, to the hands of the cardinal dean of the Sacred College of Cardinals, entrusting to him, in collaboration at least with the cardinal in charge of the dicasteries of the Roman Curia, along with the cardinal vicar of Rome (provided that they can be duly summoned; otherwise, to the cardinals who are the heads of the orders of the Sacred College), the faculty of accepting and implementing this resignation of mine

—in the Name of the Most Holy Trinity,

Rome, February 15, 1989
Ioannes Paulus PP II

John Paul II considered with lucid self-awareness the progressive deterioration of his health: "Do you think that I can't see myself, and the shape I'm in, on television?" was his reaction to one close colleague who was trying to cheer him up. When he was forced to use a cane to walk, John Paul II felt slightly embarrassed. It was painful for him to appear in public with such an unmistakable sign of his physical frailty, to the point that he had begun leaving his cane behind the door before walking onto the stage of the Paul VI Audience Hall. But he soon serenely accepted this new state, as we can see from the playful way he swung his cane in front of millions of young people on the eve of World Youth Day in Manila in January 1995.

There were also times when he tried to undercut the drama with his customary irony. On March 29, 1998, improvising during a speech, he said, "Let me ask you a question: Why does the pope carry a cane? . . . I thought you'd answer: Because he's old! Instead, you gave the right answer: Because he is a 'shepherd!' A shepherd carries a cane, to lean on and to take care of the sheepfold." On another occasion, during a trip to Latin America, he found himself in the presence of a cardinal who had suffered a mishap and had to walk with a cane. "My Dear Eminence," he said to him with a smile, "we've both been caned!"

Once he passed the age of eighty, in the year of the Great Jubilee of 2000, John Paul II abandoned himself once and for all to the hands of God. As he confided that year in his will, "I hope He will help me to recognize how long I must continue this service to which he called me on 16 October

1978. I ask him to deign to call me to Himself whenever he wishes. 'If we live, we live to the Lord, and if we die, we die to the Lord; so then . . . we are the Lord's (see Rom. 14:8). I hope that as long as I am granted to carry out the Petrine service in the Church, God in His Mercy will grant me the necessary strength for this service."

THE FATHER'S RETURN HOME

In the last month of his life, Karol Wojtyła manifested in all its transparent fullness the essence of a life spent under the auspices of "*Totus tuus*," a complete abandonment of self in the arms of the Father and the Madonna.

After undergoing a tracheotomy on February 24, 2005, to resolve an acute respiratory insufficiency, John Paul II had grave difficulty speaking. He tried to express himself with gestures to a bishop friend of his. Then, as this bishop recalled, "with a great effort he managed to say a few phrases. One was: 'It is all in the hands of God.' He was clearly serene, at peace with the situation, and aware of his condition, because he was unquestionably suffering."

During the last days he spent in the hospital, he often repeated that St. Peter had been crucified head downward. At the Gemelli Polyclinic, he had meditated daily on the death of Christ, in preparation for Holy Week. One day, the nun who was assisting him heard him ask, "What time is it?" and she replied, "Three o'clock." Whereupon the pontiff murmured,

"Oh, the Lord Jesus is already dead upon the cross, he no longer suffers," and he visibly relaxed.

On March 13, he insisted at all costs on returning to the Vatican in the hope of finding some way of celebrating the rites of Easter, but he was unable to preside over any of the ceremonies. It was a harsh blow for him. Only the previous year, when a close colleague ventured to suggest that he reduce his commitments during Holy Week, he had replied, "As long as I am alive and the Lord gives me the strength to do so, I will neglect none of the celebrations of the Mass scheduled for Holy Week and for Easter."

Millions of people around the world still cherish in their memories the image, broadcast on television, of the pope, seen from behind, in his private chapel, embracing the cross during the celebration of the Via Crucis—the Stations of the Cross—on Good Friday. Observing that scene, one privileged witness found himself remembering a similar scene, on July 17, 1991, in Comboé, in the Valle d'Aosta, during a hike: "The intense and prolonged embrace by John Paul II of a tall wooden cross standing at the edge of the alp. Watching from a respectful distance, silent and deeply moved, we saw an unexpected and disturbing sight: the pope's face was drawn with the features of a profound inner suffering."

During his last Holy Week, to a cardinal who was urging him not to strain himself excessively, he said, "Jesus did not descend from the cross, why should I?" It had already happened to him once, in Lourdes, during the pilgrimage of August 2004, that he felt himself pushed to the end of his resources. He was forced to interrupt his sermon several times, he asked his secretary for help in Polish, and when his secretary handed him a glass of water, he murmured, again in Polish, "I have to make it to the end."

On March 27, Easter Sunday, Pope Wojtyła was not even able to pronounce the words of the *Urbi et Orbi* benediction from the window looking out over St. Peter's Square, and instead was forced to do no more than make the sign of the cross with one hand. As he moved away from the window, profoundly aggrieved at his unmistakable feebleness, he uttered the most extreme words of submission to the divine will, "If I cannot perform the role of pastor, be with the people, celebrate the Holy Mass, then perhaps it is better that I die," adding immediately afterward, "Thy will be done, *Totus tuus*."

Around eleven o'clock on Wednesday, March 30, at the time of the customary general audience, he looked out of the window of the Apostolic Palace to bless the thousands of pilgrims present in St. Peter's Square: this was his last public appearance. The following day, at eleven in the morning, he was helped by his secretary priests to celebrate Mass in his private chapel; he was barely able to finish. Immediately afterward he was put to bed, and his physicians ministered to him with appropriate therapies.

On Thursday afternoon, he recited, as he was accustomed to do on that day, the Holy Hour. Then he asked to be read a passage from his book *Sign of Contradiction*, in which he commented upon a phrase spoken by Jesus, "Father, if you are willing, remove this cup from me," writing that since Christ "shares to the full the mystery of God's freedom, he knows that events do not necessarily have to take this course; but at the same time he shares God's love, and so he knows that there is no other way." He remained conscious throughout that Holy Hour and, while the litanies were being recited to Christ the priest, at the words "sacerdos et victima," he raised his hand in a gesture of consolation for a nun who he noticed was particularly moved. A little later, the situation became still more serious, with the appearance of a urinary tract infection that provoked a septic shock and a general cardiocirculatory collapse.

On Friday, April 1, Mass was celebrated at his bedside at six in the morning, and John Paul II succeeded in speaking the words of the consecration. With the aid of Sister Tobiana, he recited the hours of the breviary and the other prayers, and also performed the adoration and the meditation. Then the pope asked insistently to hear a reading of the Via Crucis and the Gospel of St. John, of which Father Tadeusz Styczeń read nine chapters.

On Saturday morning, Mass was again celebrated at his bedside, but an initial deterioration of his state of consciousness was already perceptible. He breathed very laboriously, although he was being given oxygen. In the afternoon, the rosary and vespers were recited in his bedroom.

Around eight o'clock that night, Monsignor Dziwisz decided to concelebrate Mass at his bedside. The Mass was said by Cardinal Marian Jaworski, who administered to the pope the Sacrament of the Infirm. At the moment of Communion, Dziwisz placed on his lips a small spoon with a few drops of consecrated wine. John Paul II did not open his eyes again, and he was having growing difficulty in breathing. All those present knelt in thanksgiving after the Mass and remained kneeling until the end, when Karol Wojtyła turned his head slightly to the right and his face took on a serene expression. It was 9:37 P.M. on April 2, 2005, the first Saturday of the month and the first vespers of the Feast of Divine Mercy.

Immediately the news of his death spread through St. Peter's Square. The thousands of individuals present were joined in grief, swept by the sad feeling of having just lost a beloved person who had been intensely bound up in their lives. In each of these people, however, the voice of faith recalled the extraordinary testimony that John Paul II had offered with his life, a life that was perfectly portrayed by the words of St. Paul: "I have fought the good fight, I have finished the race, I have kept the faith" (2 Timothy 4:7).

The image of the Book of the Gospel placed upon John Paul II's coffin in St. Peter's Square on the day of his funeral is now part of history: an impetuous wind, which tossed the ceremonial vestments of the cardinals at the height of the church courtyard, violently ruffled its pages. At the foot of the steps, in contrast, the air was still. The Holy Spirit was breathing around that altar. As one priest poetically commented, "At that moment I perceived not only the power of the Church orant, expressing its love and devotion to the Shepherd who had guided it for nearly twenty-seven years, but also the concrete manifestation of the Pentecost."

Less well known is another significant episode, which took place in Mexico City. Just before the funeral, the "popemobile" that Wojtyła had used during his visitations to the country was sent away from the nunciature. Inside it was the throne that he had used in one Mass, and upon the throne was placed a photograph of him. The sorrowful procession moved through the streets of the city until it reached the Basilica of the Virgin of Guadalupe, where tens of thousands of the faithful had gathered to watch the live television broadcast from Rome. The throne was placed at the entrance to the basilica and suddenly, just when St. Peter's Square was being swept by wind, a dove landed upon it.

Chapter Three

THE MYSTIC

TRAVELING UP THE RIVER
TO ITS SOURCE

A great deal has been written about the life of John Paul II. He himself told a great deal, and not only in the book-length interviews or the conversations he authorized to recall his own story, but also in the biographical fragments that he liked to insert copiously into the fabric of his essays and his speeches. Once, however, he indulged in a confidence that was quite personal: "They try to understand me from without. But I can only be understood from within."

The existential path of Karol Wojtyła in fact takes its light and its first principles from his full adherence to Christ, from his certainty of being in his hands and of never being deprived of his love. It was a spirituality expressed with extraordinary intensity by the words of St. Paul: "it is no longer I who live, but it is Christ who lives in me" (Galatians 2:20), and in it took root not only John Paul II's exercise of virtues to a heroic degree but also his ability to establish real relationships with others, in keeping with Jesus' statement "I have called you friends" (John 15:15).

His faith, his hope, and his charity, as well as his courage, his tenacity, and his detachment from worldly goods, were all nourished by his certainty that he belonged to Christ. Likewise his freedom of thought and action, as when he replied, "Oh, really? And what paper will they appear in?" to the worried colleagues who informed him about the famous photographs taken in secret by a paparazzo while he was swimming in the pool at Castel Gandolfo.

What guided his steps was his mystical capacity to observe and judge the world as the work of God and as his perennial manifestation among men—a going beyond the mere flow of things, which *Roman Triptych*, his last poetic work, translated figuratively into the enterprise of going against the current along a stream to the source, to the moment in which God created man in his own image.

This view and this closeness to Christ substantiated his priesthood. To a student at the Roman Seminary who asked him what it meant to him to be the vicar of Christ, John Paul II replied immediately and spontaneously, "Even before being the vicar of Christ, I am and I work *in persona Christi* inasmuch as I am a priest." As Pope Benedict XVI pointed out in one of his first Angeluses, the life of John Paul II can be ideally illustrated as a Eucharistic parable in which the sacrifice of himself for the Church, for his brothers, and for the glory of God was total.

He was completely willing to accept from the very outset the gift that God was offering him. At the age of just twenty, Wojtyła had already experienced the pain of physical separation from all those who were dearest to him. Left entirely alone after the death of his father, and brought intensely into touch with the unpredictability and the limits of all human certainty, he understood that he could no longer rely on his own strength, that he had to trust solely in Christ and his words of salvation. This total entrusting of self to God was certainly more than a mere compensation for a lack of intimate affections, and was in fact the natural outcome of a path he had first taken when he was very young—a path marked by the progressive discovery of the power and beauty of the word of God and its superiority to the words of men. The fundamental phase of that path was his decision to abandon the theater to enter the seminary, elevating theology over aesthetics.

BLESSED ARE THE POOR

The decision to live in communion with Christ in the name of the Truth coincided in Wojtyła with an increasingly radical orientation toward the essentials, to the poverty of spirit exalted by the first of the evangelical Beatitudes: "Blessed are the poor in spirit." Moving beyond the interpretation found in the Old Testament—which understood poverty as nothing more than the absence of material possessions, and branded it as a curse of the Lord in direct contrast to the blessings that were manifested in the form of flocks, wives, children, and wealth—Jesus, in the Sermon on the Mount, identified that poverty as the condition of those who open their heart to accept the "good news" that announces the invasion of the divine into the world, the presence of the kingdom of God among men. Karol Wojtyła's mystical path in effect took the form of a progressive transformation into one of the *anawim*, the "poor of Israel," who have no other hope, no other point of reference than God. And this was accompanied by an early ascetic abandonment of worldly goods.

Even when he worked at the Solvay plant, his fellow workers noticed that he often arrived at work in the morning without the overcoat or heavy sweater he had been wearing the day before, and he always offered the same explanation: "I gave it to someone I met on the street who needed it more than I did." They would give him something to keep him warm, but he generally kept it only for a short time, which did not fail to generate in his benefactors a certain disappointment.

After the end of the war, Wojtyła was in charge of the reception desk at the diocesan seminary on Podzamku Street. His job was to welcome and hear out all those who arrived in search of help—sometimes spiritual but far more frequently material. A former brother of his from that seminary recalled,

"Particularly edifying were his boundless faith in Divine Providence and the extraordinary sensitivity that he displayed in the face of any and all suffering. He never thought of himself or his needs. He shared all that he possessed with the poor. He knew how to give with discretion and with such respect that those who received the gift never felt humiliated. I chanced to witness these episodes through no will of my own, but I always did my best to avoid being noticed, and I crept away, to keep from causing embarrassment to him and to the recipient."

One day, the nuns where he came to celebrate Mass, now that he was a priest, noticed that he was dressed too scantily to protect him from the harsh winter chill, and decided to knit him a heavy woolen sweater. It is not difficult to imagine what they thought the next week when Father Wojtyła presented himself for Mass without the sweater, which he had given to a poor person.

One Sunday morning, in the Church of St. Florian, the faithful were obliged to wait for a good long time before he presented himself to say Mass. He was able to do so only after the sacristan, who went to see what had become of him, loaned him his own shoes. The previous evening, the young assistant parish priest had given the only pair of shoes he owned to a friend, a student who had no shoes of his own. A few years later, when he was already a bishop, during a pastoral visitation it was necessary to make an urgent purchase of a pair of shoes because the soles of the shoes he was wearing had fallen off. He still insisted on asking a cobbler's opinion, and not until the cobbler declared, "There is absolutely no way to repair these anymore!" did he resign himself to getting a new pair.

Within the diocesan curia, this sort of behavior encountered a general lack of comprehension. The archbishops who had preceded him, all of noble birth, had always ensured that the elevated level of their appearance was consistent with the authority of their position. Wojtyła constituted a sharp break with tradition. In one clear example, after a visit to a community of Polish emigrants to the United States, he received as a gift from them a brand new automobile, a deluxe Ford, which was delivered to him in person in Cracow.

The cardinal used the car for a while, then decided to replace it with a less ostentatious and cheaper Volga. His colleagues asked him the reason, and Wojtyła's answer was, "When they showed me the various models in a car catalogue, I picked the one that seemed the smallest to me. But when I saw it in real life, I realized it was too nice a car for me. And then, when I was on a pastoral visit, I heard one child say to another: 'What a car that is!' I want the faithful to remember my visits because of my ministry, not because of the car I arrived in." Of course, the money that came from trading in the luxury car for an ordinary one was donated to the poor.

THE ESSENTIAL AS A FORM OF LIBERTY

It was not easy to give him a gift. For the celebration of the twentieth anniversary of his consecration as a bishop, the diocesan prefects had decided not to give him money, because they knew he would immediately distribute any sums he received. Anyone who gave him an envelope with a cash offering could be sure that the archbishop, without even opening it, would immediately hand it over to the curia treasurer—that is, if it didn't wind up directly in the hands of a poor person first. Whenever he could, Wojtyła donated small sums to the priests who came to see him at his audiences, explaining that these were offerings for the celebration of Masses.

The chaplain of the university in Cracow remembered that, at the end of a service celebrated by the archbishop for the students in the Basilica of the Sacred Heart of Jesus, he gave him a cash offering. Wojtyła was at first reluctant to accept the offering, but in the end, after repeated and insistent urging, he acceded, saying that the sum would be used to help someone in need. A while later the chaplain learned that the money had been "returned to sender," since the cardinal had given it to the director of the university pastoral office with instructions that it be used to help poor students.

Those who were in charge of clothing him at the time remembered that Wojtyła always wore very modest apparel and refused to replace it, even when it was quite tattered. If a hole appeared, he demanded that it be patched or darned. He owned only a single overcoat, with a lining that he inserted in the winter and removed in spring and autumn. Even when he went skiing, he wore worn, old overalls, hardly adequate to protect him from the cold and damp. Basically, aside from his cassocks, his wardrobe contained only a single change of trousers and a few shirts.

One year, during a summer holiday, he took those shirts and, since it was very hot, cut off the sleeves. When winter came, his housekeeper, Maryja, realized how things stood and told the head bursar. To him the solution seemed obvious: "No problem. I'll go right now and buy him some new long-sleeved shirts." Maryja immediately objected: "It's not that simple, because he refuses to wear new clothing; he always gives it away." They went ahead and bought the shirts, but in order to get the archbishop to wear them, they had to rely on a trick that Maryja had long ago figured out: they soiled them and washed them a number of times so that they looked used. Wojtyła noticed nothing and made no objections.

Despite the fact that he had virtually no possessions, Wojtyła was always urging his housekeeper to give away anything that he felt he didn't need (even if it was a bare necessity). Every so often he would exhort her, "Go into my bedroom and clean out my personal belongings. I own too many things. Leave the more worn articles for me and give the better ones to the poor." In reality, there was never much to give away.

Once, when he was still auxiliary bishop of Cracow, Wojtyła found himself on the second story of the residence on Kanonicza Street and he heard voices from the floor below. He went downstairs to see what was happening and was told by the cook, Emilia, that a person was asking for some clothing. The bishop invited the woman to follow him to his bedroom and there he threw open his clothes closet, saying, "Please, take what you like and give it to that man." Then he returned to his work.

Once he became pontiff, Wojtyła did not temper his rigorous approach in the slightest. For example, he firmly opposed the replacement of the furniture in his Vatican apartment, furniture that had been used by Pope Paul VI and was worn and tattered; he made a concession solely for the kitchen, for considerations of safety. During a holiday in Lorenzago di Cadore, the Elizabethan Sisters, who took care of the building in which he was staying, realized that his undergarments were so patched and mended that they were irritating his skin. They took the initiative of replacing his old ones with new ones. To their surprise, they were gently scolded by the pope for having done so. He behaved the same way when he was recovering in the hospital: if the underwear he was wearing got holes in it, he asked that it be mended instead of replaced, and he invited his colleagues to distribute the new underwear to others who needed it more than he.

In this decision to live a life of complete poverty, there was nothing contrived. Karol Wojtyła acted in this way out of a desire to resemble Christ in all things. As Cardinal Camillo Ruini, vicar for the diocese of Rome during the time in which the process of beatification took place, publicly emphasized, this attitude also found its roots in the profound inner liberty that so distinguished him, and that took concrete form in his characteristic manner of relating to other people, to all of Creation, and to all material things. The testimonial that he offered was emblematic, and all the more so because it was authentically experienced at an inner level, free of the slightest ambition to make a personal impression.

Among many demonstrations is a little-known episode that happened during a pastoral visit to Brazil. When he met with the faithful in the favelas of Rio de Janeiro, John Paul II was deeply moved by the extreme poverty of one family. And so he removed the ring from his finger and gave it to the mother of the children who were crowding around him. It was the gold ring he had been given by Pope Paul VI when he was created cardinal, but he did not hesitate to give it away because, at that moment, it was the most valuable thing he possessed. And for the rest of the apostolic voyage he was obliged to borrow the episcopal ring of the cardinal secretary of state.

A CREATIVE AND POETIC
BODY OF THOUGHT

Karol Wojtyła's production of essays, nonfiction, literature, and poetry is truly vast. His so-called magisterial writing—that is, the writing he did while pope—fills dozens of volumes and, just to give an idea, is roughly twenty times the length of the entire Bible. In the context of the canonical investigation, an in-depth analysis has been performed, with the involvement of a number of experts, to identify the essential principles of that body of literature. This careful reading has produced a genuine spiritual profile of Wojtyła, with the identification—according to the judgment of one of the theologians consulted—of five areas of his thought and, therefore, of his life and his actions.

In the first place is man, immersed in a close relationship with God in Jesus Christ. It is only and exclusively in God that man can fully understand himself and it is only in God that man is capable of attaining his own vocation to happiness on earth and in heaven. A concern for the well-being of man, for his dignity and his rights—liberty, justice, and respect for life from conception to natural death—is the key theme of all the writings of the pontiff.

In second place, we find the theme of faith, as the only way in which to read and comprehend the mystery of man, of the events that occur in his life, and of the situations in the Church and in the world. Faith is also a force capable of overcoming all possible difficulties that challenge and undermine human dignity and enslave human liberty.

In accordance with his conviction that true faith comes into existence and is consolidated through love, for John Paul II the third essential aspect was charity, which consists of a heroic love for God and man. This love confers a definitive meaning on life, engenders a willingness to forgive, offers hope of a better future, and knocks down the barriers of enmity and all prejudice and hatred, laying the foundations for the civilization of love. Authentic love does not make us slaves but instead respects the liberty and the dignity of one's partner.

The fourth key theme, therefore, is dialogue, as the one and only valid and adequate form of conversation with other humans in a shared striving for truth. What gives power to this dialogue is prayer, the fifth theme, which by its very nature is a loving conversation between man and God and between God and man, the keystone of all human relations and the foundation of faith, hope, and charity.

The speeches, discourses, and documents of the pontificate of course have a special importance. Yet the most original part of Karol Wojtyła's thought can be considered to consist of his texts written outside the magisterial context, with the objective of setting down a whole series of significant reflections and ideas developed over the course of years.

What expert analysis has particularly pointed out is the creativity of his thought, combined with a deep logical discipline and a vast erudition, both philosophical and theological on the one hand and, on the other, historical and literary, with a crowning touch conferred by his distinct poetic sensibility. Among his many works, one book has been identified as the symbolic apex of his ascetic progression: *Sign of Contradiction*, a collection of the meditations in the spiritual exercises preached to Pope Paul VI and the Vatican Curia in the second week of March 1976.

The title refers to a Gospel passage, the so-called Prophecy of Simeon, concerning the newborn Jesus: "This child is destined for the falling and the rising of many in Israel, and to be a sign that will be opposed so that the inner thoughts of many will be revealed—and a sword will pierce your own soul too" (Luke 2:34–35)—a text that Cardinal Wojtyła ideally associated with Pope Paul VI, who was at the time the target of a growing ideological opposition within the Catholic Church itself. And so that series of spiritual exercises represented to Wojtyła the possibility of comforting, in his faithfulness to Christ, the successor of Peter, whose difficult task is always confirming his brothers in the faith.

As one of the theological censors explained, "The preacher returns to this theme with discretion and does so in a particularly moving manner in the 'Prayer in Gethsemane' where, in an atmosphere steeped in personal prayer, he gradually introduces the participants in the spiritual exercises to the drama of Christ's obedience to the Father and, simultaneously, to the drama of the Church, which—in the human frailty of the apostles present in the Garden of Gethsemane—failed to persevere in solidarity with Christ, who was abandoned to solitude. From that moment on, the Church was incessantly summoned by its Lord to 'recover' in a certain sense that lost hour, by a vigil of prayer that joins it in the most profound way with the Savior who is on the verge of achieving his mission of redemption."

The thorough work of analysis performed on his body of written work has made it possible to identify as underlying inspirations and motifs a number of essential traits of John Paul II's spiritual—and human—profile. Here is an enlightening summary:

1. A constant awareness of the presence of God and a wholehearted love of God.
2. A fascination with the mystery of the human person (particularly the paths of its ripening and maturing through love) and an intransigent solicitude for its salvation.
3. A strong sense of justice and a sensitivity toward the needs of those to whom a wrong has been done from a

social point of view and of those who are in danger (the unborn, the poor, the young, the sick).

4. Openness to dialogue with everyone, a willingness to take into consideration all sincere criticism and every precious contribution from others, always joined with the firm determination to announce and defend the truth: the whole truth, the unabridged truth, even when it is inconvenient and provokes opposition.

5. Respect for the diversity of vocations within the Church and the resulting necessity for collaboration, both with clergy and laity.

6. An authentic piety, firmly rooted in the Holy Scriptures and explored theologically in depth; a Trinitarian devotion, which finds its harmonious completion in Marian devotion and in the veneration of the saints.

7. A sincere love of the Church, confirmed both by his scrupulousness in understanding and studying its teachings (in particular, the teachings of the Second Vatican Council) and by diligent service to the local church of Cracow, with a simultaneous openness to assuming tasks and duties in the Universal Church.

8. An incomparable industriousness.

9. An intellectual honesty that was expressed in a sober and rigorous approach to all questions and an effort to present his own position clearly.

10. An elevated cultural level, which found expression in his style of speaking and writing.

It is in any case worth remembering that John Paul II always maintained a strong sense of humility with regard to his own publications. He obviously received countless declarations of admiration, compliments, and signs of appreciation. But he accepted them purely in the context of his mission as pontiff and not personally. One of the witnesses for the process recalled that, after the publication of the book *The Poetry of Pope John Paul II*, he heard him say wryly, "If I weren't pope, no one would be interested in these books!"

ILLUMINATING THE PATH WITH
THE FIRE OF PRAYER

The life of Karol Wojtyła was an impressive synthesis of prayer and action. It was from prayer that he derived the fertility and effectiveness of his actions. Those who were his confidants noted that John Paul II was well aware that "the pope's first responsibility toward the Church and toward the world is to pray" and that "from prayer he derived the capacity of speaking the truth without fear, since one who is alone before God has no fear of men."

In all the difficult situations of his ministry, or in particularly critical historical moments, John Paul II relied upon prayer to clarify the right path to take. When his colleagues, as they themselves have admitted, were summoned to offer possible solutions to a problem and confessed that they had no ideas, John Paul II, serene and confident, frequently comforted them with the exhortation: "We'll find something when we've prayed some more." It was not uncommon for him to gather the people who lived in the papal apartments and go with them to the chapel to pray. Once, when the circumstances were particularly dire, the pope began reciting aloud the Miserere.

When martial law was declared in Poland during the night of December 12–13, 1981, Pope Wojtyła summoned a number of Polish monsignors so they might share what they knew. One of them recalled, "We were all emotionally involved, news reports weren't getting through, we were wondering what might happen next. At the end of the dinner, as we were leaving the dining room, the Holy Father, with the greatest of tranquility, told us, 'We must pray greatly and wait for a sign from God.' Then, as was his custom, he withdrew into the chapel to pray."

He did the same thing before appointing a bishop to a diocese that was experiencing difficulties or that was particularly challenging. Just a few months before his death, he had to choose the archbishop of a major city: it was a difficult decision, because there were conflicting views in the Congregation for Bishops. The pope listened to all the information and opinions that were presented to him, and then concluded, "I will celebrate Mass for this intention, and then I will decide between the two candidates in question."

One evening, during the period of the preparation of the encyclical *Evangelium Vitae*, which was published on March 25, 1995, a very lively discussion broke out at the dinner table, with various diners eagerly defending their points of view.

The pontiff listened for almost two hours with great patience and comprehension and, at the end, said, "Very well, now you all go home and I will pray. Tomorrow I will give you my answer."

Not reserved for exceptional cases, prayer constituted the essential fountainhead from which John Paul II drew his spiritual energy in everyday life. His priestly ministry was nourished by a continuous and extraordinary contact with God, of which his preparation for the celebration of the Mass was always a part.

He began preparing for the morning services the night before, reciting in Latin the preparatory prayers. When he woke during the night, he would remember the intention for which he was to celebrate the Mass (every Wednesday, for instance, it was in support of the diocese of Rome). "When the Holy Father came to the sacristy," one of the masters of ceremonies recalled, "he would kneel or else, in the final years of his pontificate, he would sit in his chair and pray silently. The prayer would last for ten, fifteen, or even twenty minutes, and it seemed as if the pope were not present among us. At a certain point he would raise his right hand, and we would approach him to begin dressing him in absolute silence. I am convinced that John Paul II, before addressing people, addressed—or perhaps I should say, spoke with—God. Before representing him, he would ask permission to be God's living image in the presence of men. The same thing happened after he celebrated Mass: as soon as he took off his sacred vestments, he knelt in the sacristy and prayed." One witness recalled, "He was kneeling in his private chapel in an attitude of prayer.

From time to time he read something from a sheet of paper that he had before him and then he rested his forehead on his hands: it was evident that he was praying with great intensity for the intention written on that sheet of paper. Then he read something else on the same sheet of paper and resumed the attitude of prayer, and so on until he had finished, whereupon he stood up to put on his vestments."

"I am not moved during the Mass," John Paul II confided to a friend one day, "I make it happen. And I am deeply moved, both before and after." Many priests and bishops who have had the opportunity to concelebrate Mass with him have realized how true that is. "His Mass was a time of true encounter with Christ immolated and resurrected on the altar. He always celebrated with great devotion and attention. After the liturgy of the Word, he engaged in a lengthy meditation, during which there was absolute silence. The Holy Father looked at no one, he was profoundly concentrating, and the same thing happened after the Communion at the end of the Eucharistic celebration. The adoration, which lasted for a long time, never seemed particularly wearisome to anyone: one had the sensation of an otherwordly experience." And another witness summarized, "I came to the conclusion that he had an extraordinary perception of the Eucharistic mystery that he was celebrating. Above all, I was struck by the way he recited the Eucharistic prayer after the consecration: it was as if he were carrying on his shoulders the entire Church and the world." Indeed, a Muslim ambassador to the Holy See, during his farewell visit, told a friend in the Vatican, "Your Excellency, what struck me most during the three years that I have spent with you is not so much your geopolitical vision of the world, but rather having seen the pope pray in public ceremonies."

A UTILITY CLOSET AS A CHAPEL

"I am convinced that John Paul II was favored by a special grace of prayer, which allowed him to penetrate the mysteries of faith in a way that was not accessible to ordinary people," a person close to him declared. "So many times I saw his face, after contemplation and adoration, visibly changed and happy. During prayer he seemed to be in continual conversation with God, like Moses who spoke with God face to face. During prayer, Wojtyła did not notice anything that happened around him. He seemed to lose all sense of time, to the extent that his secretary at a certain point would have to shake him out of this extraordinary state of concentration because other commitments awaited him."

In contact with God, John Paul II immersed himself in a privileged dimension, practically casting off the shackles of the perception of reality. It was a mystical estrangement described by, among others, a childhood friend. One day in the early 1970s he observed that Wojtyła, young as he was, already possessed an impressive set of credentials. "Then, in all seriousness, I said that the Lord Jesus at the age of thirty-three had already 'solved' the problem of the redemption of the world. He replied, 'That was him!' and then immersed himself in prayer. The prayer lasted for a long time, it grew cold, and I said that it was time to go, but I had to wake him from that state. I have witnessed other similar situations. His was a direct conversation with God, a state of contemplation."

Even in the period when Father Karol was serving in the parish of Niegowić, the villagers noted that their young priest spent many nights before the Most Holy Sacrament, and they soon began to spy affectionately on his vigils. Often they saw him lying on the bare floor, no matter how cold it was. A Polish friend who worked in Rome was obliged to install a wooden platform over the chilly marble floor in the private chapel of the pope's Vatican apartment because Wojtyła spent hours at a time lying on the floor, his arms spread wide in the sign of the cross. Cardinal Pedro Rubiano, archbishop of Cali, was also a witness to this unusual behavior. One evening, during a pastoral visitation of Colombia, the pope said that he was tired and wished to withdraw and rest. A short while later, the cardinal went into the chapel to make sure everything was in order for the following day and found John Paul II lying there on the floor in prayer.

Certainly, logistical obstacles were never enough to discourage the pontiff when he felt within him the urgency of prayer, as is shown by several episodes of a gentle extravagance.

In May 1992, prior to the celebration of Mass at the Pordenone Fair, the pope went to the bathroom, but time passed without him returning to the space prepared as a sacristy. Concerned, one of his colleagues went to make sure everything was all right, and through the half-open door he saw John Paul II in the washroom, kneeling in prayer before a sink. Another witness, while he was at Castel Gandolfo, walked by accident into a utility closet and found the pope there rapt in prayer.

Anyone who accompanied him on a walk or a hike knew perfectly well that, once they reached their destination, they could chat for a few minutes and then he needed to be alone. Wojtyła would find a private place and meditate, contemplating nature and the greatness of God. When he went privately to the shrine of Our Lady of Mentorella, he had his driver drop him off five miles away, and then he walked up to the sanctuary, in silence, praying and meditating.

The adoration of the Most Holy Sacrament constituted for him a moment of total escape from everyday cares and an abandonment into the hands of the Lord. In Cracow, he often went to the Church of St. Joseph on Poselska Street, where a perpetual adoration is held. In the Vatican, whenever he walked by the chapel in his private apartment, he made a point of entering and pausing before the Eucharist.

During a pastoral journey, a nuncio had placed a painting by Botticelli in the chapel. At dinner, he asked the pope whether it pleased him. John Paul II replied that he had entered the chapel for the tabernacle and that no work of art, in any museum on earth, could mean more to him than that. Knowing the pope as he did, Monsignor Dino Monduzzi, when he was prefect of the papal household, always warned the organizers of papal visits not to arrange for the Holy Father to pass within view of a place where the Eucharist was kept because he was certain to enter—and spend a fair amount of time—throwing the entire day's program thoroughly out of joint.

One particularly moving event was the last celebration of Corpus Domini presided over by the Holy Father, in 2004. The pope was no longer able to walk, and his chair was fastened to the floor of the automobile that was to be used in the procession. In front of him, on the prie-dieu, the monstrance with the Most Blessed Sacrament was on display. Shortly after the departure, John Paul II spoke to a *cerimoniere*, or master of liturgical ceremonies, asking for help in kneeling. Very diplomatically, the *cerimoniere* explained that it would be too risky because the rough road made the vehicle fairly unstable. A few minutes later, the pope repeated, "I want to kneel," to which the *cerimoniere* suggested waiting for a place where the road surface was in better shape. A few moments later, however, Wojtyła exclaimed with great determination, practically shouting, "But Jesus is here. Please." It was not possible to deny him, and the two *cerimonieri* practically held him up mainly by force on the prie-dieu. Unable to support himself with his legs, the pope attempted to hold himself up by gripping the edge of the prie-dieu, but he had to be quickly settled back into his chair. It was a great display of faith: even if the body no longer responded, the will remained extremely strong.

WITH A HEART DEVOTED TO HIS HOMELAND

Prayer, an intimate dialogue with God, was for Karol Wojtyła an essential form of nourishment also in the way the rituals punctuated the days. The prayers began at five in the morning, when he went to his chapel and prayed until six. Then he returned to his bedroom for meditation before reentering the chapel at seven for Mass. The morning Act of Consecration to the Sacred Heart of Jesus constituted a vital moment of prayer for him: on a slip of now yellowed paper, which he had folded into the shape of a scapular and carried with him everywhere, John Paul II had written in his own hand in minute letters a prayer that ended with the words "*Totus tuus*, Most Sacred Heart of Jesus." At noon came the Angelus, which on Sundays he recited together with the faithful from the window overlooking St. Peter's Square, and the day ended with Compline. "He did not recite them mechanically," one nun in his entourage commented, "it was evident that he was seeking in those prayers the model and the strength to perform his duties."

The young Karol had been initiated into a love of prayer by his father, a solid, emotional point of reference for him and a guide to wisdom and spirituality during the first twenty years of his life. His father inspired in him his profound devotion to the Holy Spirit, a devotion that was reiterated daily through a prayer—only recently discovered—to which he remained faithful until the last days of his life: "Holy Spirit, I ask of you the gift of Wisdom for a better understanding of you and of your divine perfection. I ask of you the gift of Intellect for a better understanding of the essence of the mysteries of the holy faith. Give me the gift of Knowledge so that I may know how to orient my life in accordance with the principles of faith. Give me the gift of Counsel so that in all things I can seek counsel from you and can always find it in you. Give me the gift of Strength so that no fear or earthly motivations can take me away from you. Give me the gift of Piety so that I can always serve your majesty with filial love. Give me the gift of the Fear of God so that no fear or earthly motivations can take me away from you."

His father's influence was soon joined by that of the tailor Jan Tyranowski, who brought to his faith a vivid mystical impulse and familiarized him with the writings of St. John of the Cross and St. Louis-Marie Grignion de Montfort. Karol Wojtyła always felt a deep and immense sense of gratitude toward him, and once he became pope, that gratitude led him to ask a friend who was a Polish priest to begin laying the groundwork for a cause for canonization, which actually began in 1997.

His devotion had roots that were deeply sunk in Polish popular religiosity, and he remained faithful to those roots even as his own theological training and preparation deepened.

Over the course of the year, following the liturgical cycle, John Paul II was fond of returning to the traditions of his youth, such as the Christmas *Kolędy* hymns, or on Lenten Sundays the services dedicated to the Passion of Jesus with the cycle of eighteenth-century hymns called the *Gorzkie żale* (Bitter Lamentations). In the month of May, there was a Marian religious service every evening with the performance of the Lauretan litanies, while in the month of June the litanies of the Sacred Heart were sung. When the daily Mass was celebrated in Polish, it was always accompanied by chants or songs tied to the feast day or the period of the liturgical year. Those who took part pointed out that "the Holy Father knew by heart and would sing many many verses, while the others had to use their hymnals to keep up with him."

A special wave of emotion swept over him whenever he recited the Litany of the Polish Nation and the Prayer for the Fatherland by Father Piotr Skarga, with the invocations "Queen of Poland, Virgin of Jasna Góra, Virgin of Kalwaria, Virgin of Myślenice, Virgin of Rychwald, Virgin of Ostra Brama, Mother of all the Polish sanctuaries, pray for us. Mother, give strength to all those who defend life, who are at the service of life in spite of challenges, who pray for life to be respected, Mother of Sublime Love, Mother of Life and Our Hope, intercede for us."

TAKING INSPIRATION FROM THE SAINTS
FOR THE PRACTICE OF VIRTUES

Prayer and the daily practices of devotion were not neglected by the Holy Father even during his apostolic voyages. After long days of celebrations and meetings, when he returned to the nunciature, he asked his secretary for the breviary—if he had not been able to recite it already during a period of travel—and immediately went to the chapel. And if a major liturgical festivity prevented him from honoring the saint of the day, he never failed to do so at his first opportunity. He fostered a particular veneration for the saints. Every morning, when he emerged from the refectory after breakfast, he would walk through the sacristy and kiss all the relics kept on a table next to the altar. Alongside a fragment of the True

Cross of Jesus, there were displayed bodily remains of St. Peter, St. Stanisław, St. Charles Borromeo, St. Jadwiga, Queen of Poland, and many other blessed and saints. Toward the end of his life, when he was confined to a wheelchair, he continued to have his assistants take him to venerate these relics.

With the intention of offering the faithful a variegated mosaic of models to imitate, John Paul II proclaimed 483 saints and 1,345 blessed during his pontificate. In two large files, which he kept in his bedroom, he had the biographies of each of those saints and blessed, and he often spent time reading and rereading them to find inspiration for the practice of the virtues.

Among the thousands of women and men of God whom he elevated to the honor of the altars, the figure who was dearest to him was probably the Polish religious Faustina Kowalska (1905–1938), apostle of devotion to the Divine Mercy. The woman had spent much of her life cloistered in a convent, where she died at the age of only thirty-three, and Karol Wojtyła never had the opportunity to meet her. The pages of her *Diary*, with revelations of the Divine Mercy that she received directly from Jesus, however, made a deep impression upon him as a young bishop.

As he himself explained in the homily of June 7, 1997, "The Message of Divine Mercy has always been near and dear to me. It is as if history had inscribed it in the tragic experience of the Second World War. In those difficult years it was a particular support and an inexhaustible source of hope, not only for the people of Cracow but for the entire nation. This was also my personal experience, which I took with me to the

See of Peter and which in a sense forms the image of this pon-tificate." Even more emblematic was the revelation offered to the faithful on October 16, 2003, on the twenty-fifth anniver-sary of his election to the pontificate, when he emphasized, "I had to turn to Divine Mercy in order to answer the ques-tion 'Do you accept?' with confidence: 'In the obedience of faith, before Christ my Lord, entrusting myself to the Mother of Christ and of the Church, aware of the great difficulties, I accept.'"

As he explained to one of his colleagues from the Cracow years, Karol Wojtyła "believed that God's love for humanity assumes a special form in the gesture of mercy, in its haste to succor humans, sinners, the hapless, and the victims of injus-tice. He has shown us the need for a deep hope that springs precisely from an understanding of the mercy of God, and that must take a very specific, twofold form: on the one hand, it is necessary to entrust oneself to the mercy of God, and at the same time, one must have a profound sense of responsi-bility in order to be at the service of one's brothers and sisters with this mercy."

As pontiff, John Paul II dedicated his second encyclical, *Dives in misericordia*, in 1980, to the theme of God's merci-ful love, a testimonial to the powerful link that he perceived between this divine attribute and the redemption brought by Jesus Christ through his incarnation (which was the theme of his first encyclical, *Redemptor hominis*, in 1979). And the fact that Pope Wojtyła died on the evening of Saturday, April 2, 2005, when the liturgy had already begun to celebrate the feast of the Divine Mercy—which he had placed on the calendar on the Sunday after Easter, in accordance with the explicit indication provided by Jesus seventy years earlier during an apparition to Sister Faustina Kowalska—is one of those coincidences that faith teaches us to see as a divine sign, a prize to the "faithful servant."

THE PREDICTION OF PADRE PIO

Planted in the soil of this full faith in Divine Mercy was a sincere sentiment of charity toward others. At the beginning of his pontificate, John Paul II asked to have brought to him all the letters that requested any special prayer so that he could remember to mention everyone during the celebration of the Eucharist. He viewed the problems of families and individuals as his own personal matters, and he never failed to ask for information on the progress of each case.

During the general audiences, when the groups attending were named, John Paul II prayed for each of them, often giving the impression that he was aloof from the situation. In the same way, in his encounters with the crowds that gathered during his pastoral voyages, his lips moved almost imperceptibly in a silent prayer, as is clear from the television close-ups.

His loving concern for all of humanity found symbolic expression in an episode that occurred at the monastery in Tours, during his visit to France in September 1996. At the end of the meeting, to each female religious who was introduced to him he entrusted the intention of a prayer for a specific nation, thus listing all the nations of the world. As one witness observed, "There was something about him that recalled the attitude of a St. Teresa of Ávila: it was as if he were afraid of finding salvation while leaving anyone else behind to suffer eternal damnation. He hoped for the salvation of everyone, confiding in the word of Jesus, who had said, as we read in the Gospel of John, that he would draw all men unto him."

It is in this framework that we must place the powerful influence exercised on the spiritual formation of Karol Wojtyła by a great mystic of the twentieth century, Padre Pio da Pietrelcina (1887–1968), the first priest in history to have had stigmata. They were bound together by a deep relationship, as can be deduced from a letter that Wojtyła, then auxiliary bishop of Cracow, sent to Padre Pio on December 14, 1963, a letter that has only recently emerged as a result of the research conducted by the Historical Commission.

The text (which was written in Italian, and which concludes with the request for support in the pastoral situation of Cracow, quoted in the first chapter) reads: "Most Reverend Father, Your Fatherhood will certainly remember that previously on more than one occasion I have ventured to recommend to your prayers especially dramatic cases worthy of attention. I would therefore like to thank you sincerely, on the part of those in question as well, for your prayers on behalf of a woman, a Catholic physician, suffering from cancer, and the son of a lawyer in Cracow, gravely ill since birth. Both people, thanks be to God, are well. Please allow me moreover, Most Reverend Father, to entrust to your prayers a paralyzed woman in this archdiocese. At the same time, I venture to submit to you the immense pastoral difficulties that my poor efforts encounter in the present situation. I take this opportunity to reiterate my most religious expressions of respect, and it is my privilege to sign myself to your Fatherhood, most devotedly, in Jesus Christ."

Concerning the case of Dr. Wanda Półtawska, who was astonishingly cured of a cancer that, according to her physicians, she had no chance of surviving, the details were already known from an earlier letter dated November 17, 1962, in which Wojtyła asked the Capuchin priest to pray for her recovery, and a second letter dated November 28, written to inform him and thank him because, by the time she was operated upon, the tumoral mass had vanished. Nothing is known, however, of the case of the lawyer's son or of the paralyzed woman mentioned in this new letter. On the other hand, a witness to the process of beatification recounted that as early as 1957 Father Wojtyła suggested that he write to Padre Pio to ask him to pray on behalf of a seriously ill family member.

It was Commendatore Angelo Battisti, the administrative director of the Casa Sollievo della Sofferenza and an employee of the Vatican Secretariat of State, who delivered and read to Padre Pio the first missive concerning Dr. Półtawska. The Capuchin priest was outside Room 5 of the monastery. After the reading of the letter, he leaned back against the left doorpost and said happily to Battisti, "To this one I can't say no!"

Back when the young Father Wojtyła arrived in San Giovanni Rotondo in 1947 to meet him, Padre Pio had already shown an unusual attitude toward him: as he was climbing the stairs to his cell, after confession, he turned and winked to a seminarian, his spiritual son, indicating the foreign priest with a nod of the head. Some time later, speaking of the future of the Church, he described to the same seminarian a Polish pope who would be "a great fisher of men," followed by a pope "who would amply confirm the brothers" (who should be identified as the current pope, Benedict XVI).

On that occasion, Wojtyła made confession to the Capuchin priest, as he recounted on June 16, 2002, in his homily at the ceremony of canonization: "Padre Pio was a generous dispenser of divine mercy, especially through the administration of the sacrament of penance. I also had the privilege, during my young years, of benefitting from his availability to penitents." During confession, he perceived that the priest had the gift of providing spiritual guidance and later exchanged confidences with him, asking him, among other things, which of his stigmata caused him the greatest suffering. The answer was that the most painful one was on his shoulder, where Jesus had carried the cross—a stigma about which nothing was known until the death of Padre Pio, when his religious brother Fra Modestino found a shirt with a large bloodstain on the right shoulder.

One unusual episode was recounted by a witness who had an audience with John Paul II after taking part in his Mass in the private chapel. At a certain point in the conversation, he had the impression that the pontiff's face wavered and vanished, replaced by the benevolent image of the face of Padre Pio. When he revealed his experience to the pope, he heard the simple reply, "I see him, too."

IN "CONVERSATION" WITH
THE VIRGIN MARY

One can justly think that John Paul II was gifted with an extraordinary perception of the supernatural. A member of his entourage, while they were talking about Marian apparitions, asked him if he had ever seen the Madonna. The pope's response was clear, "No, I've never seen the Madonna, but I sense her."

The "partnership" of Karol with Mary actually dates back to the first minutes of his life: at the moment of his birth, on May 18, 1920, his mother in fact asked the midwife to open the window in the room so that the first sounds to greet the newborn's ears would be the chants in honor of the Madonna that wafted in just then from the nearby parish church, where the vespertine service of the Marian month was being held.

At the age of fifteen, in 1935, Karol was admitted to the Marian Congregation, but as early as 1933 he belonged to the group of candidates for admission. Later, he was elected president of the student Marian Congregation at the Marcin Wadowita boys' school in Wadowice.

From that time on, Wojtyła retained a number of external manifestations of his affiliation with the Madonna, such as the habit of keeping the crown of the rosary always wrapped around his arm by day and placed on the bed table by night, or the scapular of Our Lady of Mount Carmel hung around his neck—a scapular that was stained with his blood during the assassination attempt in 1981, and which he refused to remove, even in the operating room. His devotion already drove him, when he was studying at the Collegio Belga in the mid-1940s, to stop frequently to pray in front of Rome's so-called *madonnelle*, the votive shrines with images or bas-reliefs of the Virgin Mary. And it would later induce him, on the occasion of the Feast of the Immaculate Conception in 1981, to bless the mosaic of Maria Mater Ecclesiae (Mary Mother of the Church) newly executed on the wall of the Apostolic Palace overlooking St. Peter's Square: finally the Madonna could also appear among the many figures of apostles and saints that had for centuries adorned the Vatican basilica and Bernini's colonnade.

As Cardinal Deskur recalled, when Wojtyła was appointed archbishop of Cracow, he had found the diocesan seminary almost empty, and so he decided to make a vow to the Madonna: "I will make as many pilgrimages on foot to as many of your sanctuaries, large or small, nearby or distant, as you will give me vocations every year." Suddenly the seminary began to repopulate, and it had nearly five hundred students when the archbishop left Cracow for the throne of St. Peter. It was also in consideration of this sacred promise to the Madonna that John Paul II insisted that his pastoral travels should always include on the program a visit to at least one place of Marian worship. In Cracow, he prayed about the problems of the diocese in the nearby sanctuary of Kalwaria Zebrzydowska, which he reached by walking over footpaths, careless of the mud or the snow, to the point that his driver always made sure he had a pair of rubber boots ready in the car. After his "conversation" with the Virgin, the archbishop explained, every difficulty inexplicably found a solution.

The other Marian place "of his heart" was the Sanctuary of Częstochowa. An Italian witness who was present during John Paul II's trip to Poland recalled, "The chapel that holds the Madonna is very small. As I looked for a little room to kneel, I realized only at the last minute that I was so close to the Holy Father that I could almost touch him. He was praying. And at a certain point, he was almost praying aloud. I don't know what they said to one another. But it was a remarkable conversation! It seemed as if it would never end. That meeting with his 'mother' upset the entire schedule of the visit. And I carry with me from that journey a deep memory of that conversation. Of which I did not understand a word. Or, perhaps, I understood them all."

The intensity and the rapt concentration with which he addressed Mary conferred upon the pope, in the eyes of those who observed him, an almost supernatural aura. A guest at Castel Gandolfo during the summer holidays recalled that after regularly reciting the rosary with him in the garden, "John Paul II went over to the statue of the Madonna of Lourdes and asked me to step away, but I didn't go so far that I couldn't see. He spent at least another half hour praying there, and it was as if his person were also physically transformed." The rosary, as he himself admitted, was his favorite prayer. "Our heart can enclose in these decades of the rosary all of the facts that make up the life of an individual, a family, the nation, the Church, and all mankind. Thus the simple prayer of the rosary beats the rhythm of human life."

"After a conversation with the pope," another witness recalled, "I had the good luck, or perhaps I should say the gift, of hearing him say to me, 'We are going to recite the rosary, why don't you come with us?' I followed him onto the terrace of his apartment and so I understood the value of that rosary: a moment of vigil for his diocese, for the entire Church, for the world, and for those who suffer. 'Look!' he said, every so often between one mystery and the next, pointing out to me the various buildings of the Vatican and of Rome. At a certain point he nonplussed me by saying: 'Look, in that palazzo, that's where you live!' And then he raised his gaze toward the city. He saw everything, he knew everything. 'I know Rome better . . .' he said with a smile."

"IF I WEREN'T POPE, I WOULD ALREADY BE IN MEDJUGORJE CONFESSING"

His devoted love for Mary only grew and flourished when the connection between the third secret of Fátima and the assassination attempt of May 1981 became clear. In connection with that dramatic event, extrajudicial sources confirm, John Paul II also saw a link with the apparitions of the Queen of Peace in Medjugorje, in the former Yugoslavia, which began at the end of June of the same year. The confirmation of this link would later come, to those who believe, in the message to the faithful from Mary herself on August 25, 1994, in the period when the pope was preparing for his pastoral voyage in Croatia scheduled for the coming September 10–11: "Dear children, I am united in prayer with you today in a special way, to pray for the gift of the presence of my beloved son in your country. Pray, my children, for the health of my most beloved son who suffers, *but whom I have chosen for these times.*"

Although he never took an official position on these apparitions, in private Pope Wojtyła did not conceal his own belief. To Monsignor Murilo Sebastião Ramos Krieger, archbishop of Florianopolis in Brazil, who was going for the fourth time on a pilgrimage to the Sanctuary of the Queen of Peace, he confirmed: "Medjugorje is the spiritual center of the world!" In 1987, during a short conversation, Karol Wojtyła confided to the seer Mirjana Dragičević: "If I weren't pope, I would already be in Medjugorje confessing." This intention finds confirmation in the testimony of Cardinal Frantisek Tomasek, archbishop emeritus of Prague, who heard him say that, if he weren't pope, he would have liked to go to Medjugorje to help with the pilgrimages.

Even more eloquent in this connection are the words written black on white by the bishop of San Angelo, Texas, Monsignor Michael David Pfeifer, in a pastoral letter to the diocese on August 5, 1988: "During my visit *ad limina* with the bishops of Texas, in a private conversation with the Holy Father, I asked him what he thought about Medjugorje. The pope spoke of it in very favorable terms and said: 'To say that nothing is happening at Medjugorje means denying the living and praying testimony of thousands of people who have been there.'"

Dating back to March 26, 1984, is another episode recalled by the Slovakian archbishop, Pavel Hnilica, one of the prelates who was closest to the pontiff. When he went to have lunch with John Paul II to report to him on his secret mission to Moscow—to celebrate Mass secretly within the walls of the Kremlin—the pope asked, "Pavel, did you go to Medjugorje, then?" When Hnilica said no, because of the dissent expressed by certain Vatican authorities, the pope replied, "Go incognito and come back and tell me what you have seen." Then he took him to his private library and showed him a book by Father René Laurentin in which a number of messages from the Queen of Peace were quoted, commenting, "Medjugorje is the continuation of Fátima, it is the completion of Fátima."

After John Paul II's death, his friends Marek and Zofia Skwarnicki made available the letters that he wrote to them, abounding in specific references to Medjugorje. On May 28, 1992, the pontiff wrote to the couple: "And now every day we return to Medjugorje in prayer." Welcoming them as guests that same year for the Chrismas greeting, on December 8, he wrote on the back of the image of a saint: "I thank Zofia for everything concerning Medjugorje. I too go there every day in prayer: I am united with all who are praying there and who receive the call to prayer from there. Today we better understand this summons."

IN THE SIGN OF SUFFERING

John Paul II's distinct mystical inclination found full expression in the manner in which he lived and conceived suffering as a form of expiation and as a gift of himself to mankind. This is revealed clearly by the words that he uttered following his appendectomy in 1996: "In these days of illness I have had an opportunity once again to understand more fully the value of the service that the Lord has summoned me to render to the Church as priest, as bishop, as successor to Peter: it passes as well through the gift of suffering." In reality, a few years earlier on May 29, 1994, when he returned to the Vatican after being hospitalized for a fractured femur, he had already offered this clear-eyed analysis of his own pain: "I want to give thanks for this gift, I have understood that it is a necessary gift. The pope had to be absent from this window for four weeks, four Sundays, he had to suffer: just as he had to suffer thirteen years ago, so it is again this year."

His was truly a pontificate marked by suffering: beginning with that dramatic May 13, 1981, John Paul II spent no fewer than 164 days at the Gemelli Polyclinic, which he ironically dubbed "Vatican Number 3," after St. Peter's Square and Castel Gandolfo. Along with the first twenty-two days following the attempted assassination, there were another fifty-six days between June and August of that year, to treat a cytomegalovirus infection and to perform a new round of surgery. There were four more stays in the hospital in succession about ten years later: fifteen days in 1992 for the removal of a benign tumor from the intestine; two days in 1993 for a dislocated right shoulder, which he was obliged to have strapped up for a month; thirty days in 1994 for the fracture of his right femur after a fall in the bathroom; ten days in 1996 for the removal of his appendix. His last two stays in the hospital, for a total of twenty-eight days in February and March 2005, were to perform a tracheotomy when an acute laryngotracheitis made independent breathing very difficult.

Every physical problem was for him a reason for personal meditation: "I ask myself what God is trying to tell me with this disease," he replied to a doctor who asked how he was feeling. But aside from the significance to be attributed to his own suffering, it was the suffering of mankind that offered Pope Wojtyła a theme for special reflection, to which he dedicated in February 1984 the apostolic letter *Salvifici doloris* (The Salvific Power of Pain). In mid-December 1997 in remarks to two papal audiences, the pontiff touched on the same theme, confirming the redeeming value of suffering with the human story of Jesus, whose coming to earth, "with all the joy it involves for humanity, is inseparably linked to suffering," and declaring that in Christ "pain receives a new light, which elevates it from simple and negative passivity to positive collaboration in the project of salvation," and that, in the dimension of the Gospel, suffering "is not wasted energy, because it is transformed by divine love."

Without ignoring the importance of his own theological reflections on the topic, the words he confided to a friend express his full awareness of the incomparable value that suffering assumes when someone takes it upon himself: "I have

written many encyclicals and many apostolic letters, but I
realize that it is only with my suffering that I can best help
mankind. Think of the value of pain, suffered and offered
with love. . . ." During a celebration in St. Peter's, one of the
cerimonieri noticed the grave expression of pain on the pontiff's face and asked him, "Your Holiness, can I do anything
to help? Is something causing you pain?" And he replied, "By
now, everything causes me pain, but that is how it must be."

Giving meaning to pain did not mean to Pope Wojtyła
that we need not do all we can to alleviate it and bring comfort to those who are suffering. If "the Cross is the first letter
of God's alphabet," as he stated, that does not mean that the
Christian dimension of suffering "is reduced only to its profound significance and its character of redemption." Pain, in
fact, must "generate solidarity, dedication, and generosity in
all those who suffer and in all those who hear the summons
to attend them and aid them in their suffering"—an appeal
intended for all men, inasmuch as "no institution by itself
can replace the human heart, human compassion, when one
wishes to bring succor to physical suffering." That is why he
decided to attend the World Day of the Sick, instituted at his
initiative in 1992 and since then celebrated every February
11, in conjunction with the liturgical commemoration of Our
Lady of Lourdes, an opportunity to meditate on pain, but also
to urge solidarity with those who suffer.

THE STATIONS OF THE CROSS
IN THE HALLWAY

When it was not some infirmity or other that caused him to experience pain, it was he himself who inflicted discomfort and mortification on his own body. Aside from the prescribed fasting, which he followed with great rigor, especially during Lent, when he reduced his nourishment to one complete meal a day, he also abstained from food before ordaining priests and bishops. And it was not infrequent for him to spend the night lying on the bare floor. His housekeeper in Cracow realized it, even though the archbishop rumpled his bedclothes to conceal it. But he did more. As a number of members of his closest entourage heard with their own ears, in Poland and in the Vatican, Karol Wojtyła flagellated himself. In his bedroom closet, among his cassocks, hanging from a hook was an unusual trouser belt that he used as a whip and always brought to Castel Gandolfo.

This practice was not an expression of Wojtyła's wish to inflict punishment on his own body, which was a gift of God. Instead, it fit into a larger Christian tradition, especially into the asceticism of the Carmelite order—they often prayed the Miserere while holding their arms in the sign of the cross, and flogged themselves with the sashes of their monastic cassocks. He remained faithful to that tradition throughout his life. As Cardinal Carlo Maria Martini wrote in response to this same report, "In asceticism, one practices minor acts of penitence, which do not cause lasting bodily harm; therefore, we should not think of them as instances of self-mutilation or masochism."

"I am now rejoicing in my sufferings for your sake, and in my flesh I am completing what is lacking in Christ's afflictions for the sake of his body, that is, the Church," in the words of St. Paul in Colossians 1:24. Karol Wojtyła made these words a foundation of his own testimonial of faith. When he was suffering greatly, for instance in the aftermath of surgery, he said, "Restitution must be made. How much Our Lord Jesus had to suffer." He said the same words in the final hours of his illness, when he was thirsty but could not be given anything to drink.

The Calvary of Christ, by the light of which he considered his own suffering, was symbolically renewed by the pontiff every Friday with the practice of the Via Crucis, the Stations of the Cross. In the Vatican, Wojtyła celebrated it in his private chapel, or else on the terrace above the papal apartments, which was transformed over time into an authentic open-air chapel, adorned with flowers and plants. In the chapel at Castel Gandolfo, however, there were no stations and so, during the summer holidays, every Friday the pontiff secretly went to pray before the fourteen lithographs featuring reproductions of the Via Crucis that he had discovered by chance in a hallway near the dining room, not normally in use.

During a pastoral journey, a person in his entourage realized how deep-seated the pope's faithfulness was to this practice of devotion: "We were in the helicopter that was taking us from Jerusalem to Galilee, and it was a Friday. I noticed that the pope was not looking out the window, but was holding in his hand a book without a cover. He would read a page and then engage deeply in prayer, then he would read another page and begin praying again. I looked over and realized that he was doing the Via Crucis, because that day, since there was a very heavy schedule ahead, he was afraid he would not be able to do it in the chapel as was his custom."

His was a faithfulness that remained solid to the very end. The day before he died, April 1, 2005, around ten in the morning, John Paul II tried to communicate to the people near him something that they could not understand. His raging fever, his difficulty in breathing, made it almost impossible for him to articulate words. And so he was brought a pen and a sheet of paper, upon which the pope wrote that, since it was Friday, he wanted to do the Via Crucis. One of the nuns who was present therefore began to read it aloud while he, with some difficulty, traced the sign of the cross every time that one of the stations began.

Epilogue

A TRIBUTE TO THE TRUTH

On April 2, 2005, I was in St. Peter's Square, together with thousands of the faithful. When at 9:37 P.M. the news of the death of John Paul II was announced, I felt a growing desire inside myself to shout out, "The saint is dead!" just as the children of Rome had done in the late eighteenth century as they ran through the streets broadcasting the news of the demise of St. Benedict Joseph Labre. Part of me, perhaps, believed that if that shout swelled into a mass chorus, if all the faithful gathered there that day joined me in that outcry, his canonization would simply be accepted by acclamation. The luminous testimony of faith offered to the world over the course of the years by John Paul II, his possession and practice of all the virtues at the highest levels, the decision to bear upon his own shoulders the cross of suffering until the end of his days, his deeply caring love for his fellow man—all these were now intrinsic traits of his figure as a man and as a pastor, and they certainly argued strongly in favor of his immediate induction into the ranks of the saints.

Instead, I remained silent, and I admit that now I regret it somewhat. Still, I am convinced that going through the process has been very useful: it was quite different from a bureaucratic examination of a life, certainly not a dull "reckoning" of his merits under a chilly and inquisitorial glare. Quite the contrary: it allowed us to restore the intensity and vigor of the already well-known aspects of the human life of Pope Wojtyła, inlaying it with the weave of previously unknown episodes offered to the rest of us by those who have preserved them in memory.

Many of the faithful felt they were summoned by the message of the edict promulgated by Cardinal Camillo Ruini on May 18, 2005, the day that Wojtyła would have turned eighty-five if he had lived. With that appeal, His Holiness's vicar for the diocese of Rome invited the faithful to "communicate all reports from which it is possible to determine evidence favorable or contrary to the reputation for saintliness of the Servant of God" and "to submit any and all writings that were authored by the Servant of God." On June 28 of that year, the eve of the feast day of Saints Peter and Paul, Apostles, the opening session was held of the diocesan investigation into the life, virtues, and reputation for saintliness of Pope

Wojtyła. A few months later, the new archbishop of Cracow, Cardinal Stanisław Dziwisz, offered to the Polish faithful the same opportunity to provide testimony, inaugurating the rogatory phase of the diocesan process on November 4, the feast day of St. Charles Borromeo and therefore the name day of the pope. To the rogatory processes of Rome and Cracow was added another in New York, to gather the testimony of a United States citizen.

A total of 114 persons were heard: 35 cardinals, 20 archbishops and bishops, 11 priests, 5 religious, 3 nuns, 36 lay Catholics, 3 non-Catholics, and a Jew. Their declarations, along with other documents and writings, filled the thousands of pages of the so-called *Copia Pubblica*, from which were drawn the four condensed volumes of the *Positio*. These are substantial numbers. Besides the statements gathered in the context of the tribunal, there were also the declarations made in countless letters sent by the faithful to the Postulatio. Many of these, especially those written in the immediate aftermath of the death of John Paul II, express sincere gratitude to God for the gift of this great pope. Others contain moving attestations to graces received, setting forth cases of spiritual or physical healing attributed to the intercession of Pope Wojtyła.

To gather and evaluate all this material, as well as to listen to the witnesses who took part in this process, has been for me and for my colleagues a truly demanding job. Without doubt, it was also indispensable, for it allowed us to corroborate the reputation for saintliness of John Paul II, providing a precious tribute to the truth. A truth that, thanks to the voices of those who have helped to preserve it intact, now shines incontestable and brilliant.

For further information and to organize meetings on the topic, the authors can be contacted at the e-mail addresses papa-gp2@ virgilio.it and papa-gp2@libero.it.

CONCISE CHRONOLOGY OF
THE LIFE OF KAROL WOJTYŁA—
JOHN PAUL II

On May 18, 1920, Karol Józef Wojtyła is born in Wadowice, Cracow Province, Poland, to the forty-year-old army officer Karol Wojtyła and Emilia Kaczorowska, a thirty-six-year-old housewife. He has a brother, Edmund, fourteen years older, while a sister, Olga, died in infancy six years before. He is baptized on June 20, 1920.

On September 15, 1926, he begins attending elementary school.

On April 13, 1929, his mother dies of heart disease, and on December 5, 1932, his brother, now a doctor, also dies, victim of a scarlet fever epidemic.

On May 3, 1938, he receives confirmation, and in the same month he passes the final exams of the *liceum*. On June 22, he enrolls in the Department of Philosophy at the Jagiellonian University, and he and his father soon move to Cracow. Here, in February 1940, he makes the acquaintance of Jan Tyranowski, who puts him in contact with the Living Rosary group and introduces him to the study of mysticism. On November 1 of that year, he begins working in the Zakrzówek stone quarry to avoid deportation to Germany, which has occupied Poland for the past year.

On February 18, 1941, his father dies, and in August he welcomes into his house the family of Mieczysław Kotlarczyk, the founder of the Theater of the Living Word. During the spring of 1942, Karol takes a job at the Solvay plant, and in October he begins to attend the clandestine courses of the Department of Theology at the Jagiellonian University as a seminarian. In March 1943, he makes his last appearance on the stage, as the star of Juliusz Słowacki's play *Samuel Zborowski*. On February 29, 1944, he is hit by a truck and admitted to the hospital. In August of that year, Archbishop Sapieha has him move, together with the other clandestine seminarians, to the archbishop's palace in Cracow.

On November 1, 1946, he is ordained a priest in the private chapel of Cardinal Sapieha. On November 15, he leaves for Rome to continue his theological studies at the Pontifical University of St. Thomas Aquinas (Angelicum). On July 3, 1947, he passes his final examination in theology, and during the summer he travels to France, Belgium, and the Netherlands. On June 19, 1948, he defends his dissertation, "Doctrina de fide apud S. Ioannem a Cruce" (The Doctrine of Faith According to St. John of the Cross), and a couple of weeks later he returns to Cracow.

On July 8, 1948, he is assigned to the parish of Niegowić as assistant parish priest. On December 16, the Jagiellonian University officially awards him the academic title of doctor in theology. In August 1949, he is appointed assistant parish priest at St. Florian's in Cracow.

On September 1, 1951, the archbishop of Cracow, Eugeniusz Baziak, gives him a two-year leave of absence to study and qualify as a university professor. In October 1953, he begins teaching Catholic social ethics in the Department of Theology at Jagiellonian University, and in December he is certified for teaching. In 1954, he becomes a professor at the Cracow seminary and at the Catholic University of Lublin. On November 15, 1957, he is appointed a full professor by the Central Credentials Commission.

On July 4, 1958, he is appointed auxiliary bishop in Cracow, and on September 28 he receives the episcopal consecration as bishop.

In 1960, he publishes his book *Love and Responsibility*.

Following the death of Archbishop Baziak, on July 16, 1962, he is elected vicar capitular. On October 5, he leaves for Rome, where from October 11 to December 8 he participates in the first session of the Second Vatican Council. Again, in Rome, from October 6 to December 4, 1963, he participates in the second session of the Second Vatican Council, and from December 5 to 15 he makes a pilgrimage to the Holy Land.

On December 30, 1963, he is appointed archbishop of Cracow. On January 13, 1964, the official bull is published with his appointment, and on March 8 his solemn installation is celebrated in the Wawel Cathedral. From September 14 to November 21, he participates in the third session of the Second Vatican Council in Rome, and immediately afterward goes again on a two-week pilgrimage to the Holy Land. From September 14 to December 8, 1965, he participates in Rome in the fourth and final session of the Second Vatican Council. From April 13 to 20, 1967, he takes part in Rome in the first meeting of the Council for the Laity.

On June 28, 1967, he receives the title of cardinal from Pope Paul VI.

In 1969, he publishes the essay *The Acting Person*, and from October 11 to 28 he takes part in Rome in the first extraordinary general assembly of the Synod of Bishops. In 1972, he publishes his study of the implementation of the Second Vatican Council, *Sources of Renewal*, and on May 8 he opens the Synod of the Archdiocese of Cracow. From March 2 to 9, 1973, he participates in the Eucharistic Congress in Australia, and also visits the Philippines and New Guinea. That same year, he travels in May to Belgium and in November to France.

From September 27 to October 26, 1974, he takes part in Rome in the third ordinary general assembly of the Synod of Bishops, at which he is the speaker for the doctrinal section. From March 3 to 8, 1975, in Rome, he participates in the first meeting of the Council of the General Secretariat of the Synod of Bishops, and in September he travels to the German Democratic Republic. From March 7 to 13, 1976, he preaches the spiritual exercises in the Vatican in the presence of Pope Paul VI; the meditations will be published in the volume *Sign of Contradiction*. From July 23 to September 5, 1976, he travels in the United States and Canada, delivering a number of lectures as well.

In 1978, from August 11 to September 3, he is in Rome for the funeral of Pope Paul VI, the Conclave, and the ceremonies following the election of the new pope, John Paul I. On October 3, he is again in Rome for the funeral of John Paul I. On October 14, he enters the Conclave, and on October 16, around 5:15 P.M., he is elected pontiff, taking the name John Paul II. On October 22, he celebrates the solemn beginning of his ministry as Supreme Pastor of the Catholic Church. On November 5, he goes on a pilgrimage to the basilica at Assisi and to the Roman basilica of Santa Maria sopra Minerva to venerate the patron saints of Italy, St. Francis and St. Catherine. On November 12, he takes possession, as bishop of Rome, of the throne at St. John Lateran.

On March 4, 1979, his first encyclical, *Redemptor hominis*, is published. In June, he returns to Poland on a pastoral visit. In October, he addresses the United Nations in New York, and in November he meets with the Orthodox patriarch Dimitrios I in Turkey. On Good Friday, April 4, 1980, for the first time he confesses a number of the faithful in the Vatican basilica. On November 30, the encyclical *Dives in misericordia* is published. On January 11, 1981, he begins the custom of baptizing children in the Vatican during the Epiphany season.

At 5:19 P.M. on May 13, 1981, in St. Peter's Square, he is the victim of an assassination attempt by Ali Ağca. He undergoes emergency surgery at the Gemelli Polyclinic, and after three weeks, returns to the Vatican on June 3, but is again hospitalized from June 20 to August 14.

In 1982, in May, he goes on a pilgrimage to Fátima to thank the Madonna for her maternal protection and to recite, one year after the assassination attempt, the Act of Consecration of the World to the Immaculate Heart of Mary. On October 10, he presides over the ceremony of canonization of Father Maximilian Kolbe. In 1983, on January 25, he promulgates the new Code of Canon Law, on March 25 he opens the Holy Year of Redemption, and on December 27 he visits Ali Ağca in the Roman prison of Rebibbia. He closes the Holy Year of Redemption on April 22, 1984.

On March 30 and 31, 1985, he welcomes to Rome the participants of the international gathering of young people for World Youth Day. In 1986, he visits the Synagogue of Rome on April 13. On May 18, the encyclical *Dominum et vivificantem* is published. On October 27, in Assisi, he presides over the World Day of Prayer for Peace. In 1987, on March 25, the encyclical *Redemptoris Mater* is published. On the eve of Pentecost, on June 6, he opens the Marian Year. On December 30, the encyclical *Sollicitudo rei socialis* is published.

In 1988, on May 21, he inaugurates in the Vatican the Dono di Maria shelter, entrusted to the congregation of Mother Teresa of Calcutta. On June 28, he signs the apostolic constitution *Pastor Bonus* for the reform of the Roman Curia. On August 15, he closes the Marian Year. In 1989, he inaugurates the Day of Prayer for Peace in Lebanon on September 7, and on September 30 he receives a visit from Robert Runcie, archbishop of Canterbury and head of the Church of England. In

1990, on August 26, he launches an appeal for peace in the Persian Gulf, after the Iraqi invasion of Kuwait. On December 7, the encyclical *Redemptoris missio* is published.

In 1991, he sends a letter on January 15 to U.S. president George Bush and Iraqi president Saddam Hussein to try to prevent the Gulf War. On May 1, the encyclical *Centesimus annus* is published. In 1992, from July 12 to 26, he is hospitalized at the Gemelli Polyclinic of Rome for an operation to remove a benign intestinal tumor. On December 9, the Catechism of the Catholic Church, already approved in June, is made public. In 1993, on January 9 and 10, he presides over a special prayer meeting in Assisi for peace in Europe and especially in the Balkans. On August 6, the encyclical *Veritatis splendor* is published. On November 11, he slips and sprains his right shoulder, which is immobilized for a month.

On January 23, 1994, he celebrates in the Vatican basilica a Mass for peace in the Balkans. On April 28, he falls and fractures his right femur; he undergoes an operation at the Gemelli Polyclinic and remains hospitalized until May 27. On November 14, the apostolic letter *Tertio millennio adveniente* is made public, with the announcement of the Jubilee of 2000. In 1995, the encyclicals *Evangelium vitae* is published on March 25, and it is followed by the publication of the *Ut unum sint* on May 25. In 1996, with the apostolic constitution *Universi dominici gregis* published on February 22, he reforms the rules for the Conclave. From October 6 to 15, he is hospitalized at the Gemelli Polyclinic for an appendectomy.

In 1997, on June 16, he sends a letter to Israeli prime minister Benjamin Netanyahu and Palestinian Authority president

Yasser Arafat urging peace in the Middle East. In 1998, the encyclical *Fides et ratio* is published on September 14, while on November 29 the bull *Incarnationis mysterium* is made public, ordering the Jubilee of 2000. In 1999, with the apostolic letter *Spes aedificandi* dated October 1, he proclaims as joint patron saints of Europe three female saints—Bridget of Sweden, Catherine of Siena, and Edith Stein (Teresa Benedetta della Croce). On the night of December 24, the great Jubilee of 2000 is inaugurated.

In 2000, he goes on a pilgrimage to Mount Sinai in Egypt from February 24 to 26 and to the Holy Land (Jordan, autonomous Palestinian territories, and Israel) from March 20 to 26. On May 7, he presides over the Ecumenical Commemoration of Witnesses to the Faith in the Twentieth Century." On May 12 and 13, he makes a pilgrimage to Fátima, where the revelation of the "third secret" is announced. In 2001, on January 6, he closes the Jubilee of 2000 and signs the postjubilee apostolic letter *Novo millennio ineunte*. In 2002, on January 24 in Assisi, he presides over the Day of Prayer for Peace in the World. On October 16, with the apostolic letter *Rosarium Virginis Mariae*, he proclaims the Year of the Rosary and adds the five "luminous" mysteries to the traditional Marian prayer. On March 5, 2003, he presides over a Day of Prayer and Fasting for Peace.

On April 23, 2003, completing 8,959 days of pontificate, he becomes the third longest-lived pope in history (after Pius IX and Leo XIII, and leaving aside the case of St. Peter). On April 17, the encyclical *Ecclesia de eucharistia* is published. On October 16, he presides over the solemn concelebration of the

Mass, marking the twenty-fifth anniversary of his election to the pontificate.

In 2004, on February 28, after personally visiting 301 Roman parishes from the beginning of his pontificate, he receives, in the Vatican, a group of representatives of the rest. On June 10, he announces the celebration of a special Year of the Eucharist. On August 14 and 15, he goes on a pilgrimage to Lourdes and on September 5 to Loreto: these are his last two voyages.

On January 30, 2005, he recites for the last time in person the Sunday Angelus. In the evening of February 1, he is hospitalized at the Gemelli Polyclinic with a respiratory crisis. On February 10, he returns to the Vatican, but on February 24 he is readmitted to the Gemelli Polyclinic and remains hospitalized until March 13 because of a relapse of the previous flu syndrome. On March 30, at the hour of the general audience, he looks out the window in the Apostolic Palace to bless the thousands of pilgrims present in St. Peter's Square: this is his last public appearance. On the afternoon of March 31, he develops a urinary tract infection that causes septic shock with cardiocirculatory collapse. He dies at 9:37 P.M. on April 2, the first Saturday of the month and the first vespers of the Feast of the Divine Mercy. He has lived 84 years, 10 months, and 15 days and has been pope for 26 years, 5 months, and 17 days.